Kay Coy

Art Activities For Anytime

A collection of art activities
from *The Mailbox*® magazine

Editors:
Becky Andrews
Lynn Bemer
Diane Badden
Irving Crump
Sarah McCutcheon
Karen Shelton
Kathy Wolf

Artists:
Pam Crane
Teresa Davidson
Rebecca Saunders
Jennifer Tipton

Table Of Contents

©1990 by THE EDUCATION CENTER, INC.
All rights reserved except as here noted.

ISBN# 1-56234-013-1

Except as provided for herein, no part of this publication may be reproduced or transmitted in any form or by any means, electronic or mechanical, including photocopying, recording, or storing in any information storage and retrieval system or electronic on-line bulletin board, without prior written permission from The Education Center, Inc. Permission is given to the original purchaser to reproduce patterns and reproducibles for individual classroom use only and not for resale or distribution. Reproduction for an entire school or school system is prohibited. Please direct written inquiries to The Education Center, Inc., P.O. Box 9753, Greensboro, NC 27429-0753. The Education Center®, *The Mailbox*®, and the mailbox/post/grass logo are registered trademarks of The Education Center, Inc. All other brand or product names are trademarks or registered trademarks of their respective companies. Printed in the United States of America.

Manufactured in the United States
10 9 8 7 6 5

- Adapt ideas in this book to go with a particular season, holiday, or theme. For example, make colorful heart decorations in February using the technique given in the October activity, "Pumpkin Decoration" on page 22.

- Get parents and students involved in helping you collect art supplies from home. Duplicate the reproducible letter on page 4 to send home at the beginning of the year. Before duplicating, place a check beside items you will need for your art program and add your signature.

- Don't have time each week for a whole-class art lesson? Many of the ideas in this book are very simple and perfect for independent projects. Place supplies and instructions at an art center. Assign several students to be your art helpers. Rather than interrupt you while you are working with groups, students can take their questions about the art center activity to one of the special helpers. Don't forget to recognize your special helpers with the reproducible award on page 5.

- Have you ever wanted to do a classroom art activity, but you didn't have enough of one item? Put a sample of the needed item and the number you want on a Wanted Sign outside your door. Post a daily count of how many you have collected to avoid an overflow.

- Check at your local printing shop for leftover and scrap paper available for teachers. You'll probably find pieces in all colors, sizes, and weights. Stock up on large and small scraps to make flash cards and games as well as art projects.

- Install a cafe curtain rod as a dispenser for a big roll of shelf or freezer paper in your art center. Hang a pair of blunt-nosed scissors nearby so that children can help themselves.

- To make chalk art pieces easier to work with, dip chalk into sugared water before drawing. Finished art will not smear.

- Make paint containers large enough for several students to use. Cut plastic milk containers (half-gallon or gallon) about two inches from the bottom. To reuse, simply rinse them out.

Art Tips

- Is a squirt of tempera paint all you need? Save plastic, squirt-top, liquid detergent bottles. Mix tempera paints at the beginning of the year, and store them in these clean bottles. You'll save time when paint is needed for art projects or small touch-ups.

- Don't throw away old brushes from fingernail polish bottles. Clean them in nail polish remover and use as paintbrushes for those hard-to-reach places.

- Here's another use for old fingernail polish bottles. Use empty ones to store glue. The small brush prevents children from getting too much glue on their projects, and that saves on your glue!

- Clean up sloppy painting times with empty roll-on deodorant bottles. Fill with thinned tempera paint and use on large pieces of paper. Remind children to shake the bottles often—with the caps on!

- Plastic, six-pack drink holders make great mobiles. Tie a string to each ring and attach your pictures. They're much softer and lighter than coat hangers.

- Keep a can of laundry soap flakes by the sink for easy washup after art activities. Instruct children to place one finger in the flakes before washing. It takes less time and less soap, and results in less mess.

- An easy way to get those dirty worktables clean is to let children finger paint on the tabletops with shaving cream. They'll have loads of fun, the tables will be clean, and the room will have a good, fresh smell.

- Wipe out sticky hands during activities requiring glue. Keep a damp sponge at each worktable to clean messy hands. This technique eliminates disruptive traffic to and from the sink.

- Use monofilament fishing line under the chalkboard for displaying artwork. Run the line through the center springs of short, colored clothespins to have a handy way to hold up work.

- To display children's artwork, cover three boxes of graduated size with fabric or Con-Tact paper. Stack the boxes; then staple flat artwork to the sides. Use the top of the pyramid for three-dimensional artwork.

Dear Parent,

Can you help us? Our class needs the art supplies indicated below. Please send any available materials to school with your child.

_____	egg cartons	_____	Styrofoam meat trays
_____	pipe cleaners	_____	fabric scraps
_____	empty nail polish bottles	_____	newspapers
_____	cotton balls	_____	yarn
_____	ribbon	_____	sponges
_____	wallpaper samples	_____	glitter
_____	buttons	_____	paper plates
_____	empty liquid detergent bottles	_____	tubes from paper towels, toilet tissue, gift wrap
_____	sandpaper		
_____	baby food jars	_____	Popsicle sticks
_____	gift wrap	_____	old greeting cards
_____	paper towels	_____	paper or plastic bags
_____	empty plastic milk containers	_____	empty plastic liter bottles
_____	plastic drinking straws	_____	plastic wrap
_____	old magazines or catalogs	_____	aluminum foil
_____	clothespins	_____	waxed paper

Other: _____

_____

Thank you!

©1990 The Education Center, Inc.

Note To Teacher: Before duplicating, check the items you need, add any others not on the list, and sign your name. Send home with
4 students at the beginning of the year or any time supplies are needed.

What a work of art,

_____
student

Your creativity is dazzling!

Congratulations!

_____
teacher

_____
date

Fantastic!

Amazing!

Wow!

©1990 The Education Center, Inc.

There's no doubt about it!

_____
student

helped make our art class a success!

Thanks for your help!

_____
teacher

_____
date

©1990 The Education Center, Inc.

Fall

Disco Names

Getting acquainted inspires fun with fancy name art. Have each child write his or her name on a piece of white paper with a marker. Students then go around their names with crayons. Each student continues to outline around his name with different colors until his paper is filled up. Display the names where students can get up close to examine them. Every unique name design is a reminder that every classmate is unique!

Friendship Rainbow

Join hands to make a friendship rainbow! Cooperation creates a cheerful bulletin board or wall decoration. Give each child a piece of 8 1/2" x 11" white paper and a specific color to paint. Children work in pairs. One child paints his partner's hands and helps to press painted hands onto the paper. When both children have made handprints and the paint is dry, the prints are cut out and mounted with others in the form of a rainbow.

Me Mobiles

Get to know your students through this art project. Give each child a 12" x 18" piece of construction paper to fold into thirds. Each student uses markers or crayons to write his name and a describing word in one section. He draws what he likes to do in another section and what he wishes he could do in the future in the third one. Fasten paper in a triangular prism shape, add string, and suspend.

©1990 The Education Center, Inc.

Fit To Be Tied

Establish your class identity with a fashion statement! Everyone in the school will recognize your students when they're wearing their very own tie-dyed, T-shirt originals.

Materials:

one color of liquid Rit dye
cold water in classroom sink
1 cup of salt per bottle of dye
plastic dishpan
plastic drop cloth or newspapers

scissors
clothes hangers
white, cotton T-shirts
heavy, waxed thread
plastic gloves

Procedure:

1. Place drop cloth or newspapers on work area. Have a source of clear water or a sink with a drain nearby. Mix dye in dishpan of cold water according to package directions.

2. Dissolve the salt in hot water and add to dye bath. (This will help set the color since cold water is being used.)

3. Show each student how to prepare his shirt by poking a finger up through one layer of fabric. Remove finger and wrap the cloth bundle tightly with many turns of thread. (The more turns of thread the wider the design.) Wrap several bundles using this procedure.

4. Before immersing each T-shirt in the dye bath, thoroughly wet it and remove excess water.

5. Wearing plastic gloves, place several T-shirts in the dye bath for 10–15 minutes. Remove and rinse each shirt until water is clear. (Make sure children wash their hands thoroughly after dyeing to remove toxins.)

6. Unwrap or cut threads with scissors. Hang shirts to dry on a clothesline or on clothes hangers.

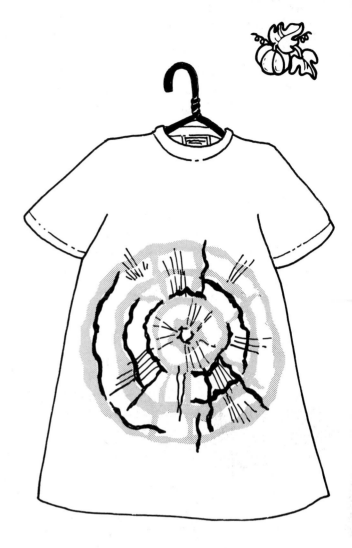

Three-Dimensional Picture Frames

Expand bulletin board displays to three dimensions. Have children make their own attractive picture frames for their artwork. For a picture less than 9" x 12", take a piece of 9" x 12" construction paper, and fold once. Cut as shown. (Pinking shears or scalloping scissors make interesting edges.) Open up the paper, and with a felt-tipped pen, outline each cut edge. Turn paper over; then paste back each triangular shape. Staple a picture or child's artwork to a piece of oaktag. Then staple the frame on top for a work of art. Each student can proudly say, "I framed it myself!"

Fold

©1990 The Education Center, Inc.

"Hoop-la!"

Do your classroom windows lack visual appeal? Add splashes of color at your windows to reflect a rainbow of seasonal moods. For each of these projects you'll need several embroidery hoops and cellophane which is available in a variety of colors from art supply stores. (The use of "Easter basket" cellophane is not recommended. And acetate, which makes lovely projects, is too expensive for this purpose.)

To decorate your classroom windows for September, you'll need red cellophane (or tissue paper), monofilament line, cuphooks, embroidery hoops, glue, scissors, and green construction paper. In preparation for hanging your projects, attach cuphooks above each of your windows. To convert your supplies into gorgeous red apples, stretch red cellophane across each hoop, trim, and fasten snugly. Glue a green construction paper leaf near the top of each hoop. Attach lengths of monofilament line to the tops of hoops, and make a loop in the top of each line for hanging. Suspend these eye-catching apples from the cuphooks for a razzle-dazzle display.

Each month thereafter, substitute different colors of cellophane or experiment with tissue paper, foils (for the holidays), doilies, waxed paper, and different construction paper add-ons to give your classroom vastly different looks.

©1990 The Education Center, Inc.

Decorative Artwork Carriers

Students will love this unique and fun way to carry artwork home! Have students decorate and label paper towel tubes brought from home. Periodically have students roll up their completed projects and place them inside their tubes.

Sponge Printing

Sponge printing is a fun and easy way to introduce children to printmaking. Using tempera paint, paint a picture directly onto a jumbo sponge. Pick up the sponge and press it, painted side–down, onto a sheet of paper. Just rinse the sponge, and it's ready for the next student. Not only is this type of printing much easier for young children, but the sponge also soaks up excess paint, eliminating runs. You can also use this process to decorate brown handy bags from The Education Center for Halloween.

Oval Frames

Turn your students' artwork into a professional-looking display. Cut ovals in 12" x 18" sheets of black construction paper. Place the frames over student artwork on bulletin boards or walls. Add name tags to finish the display. Your students will marvel at this elegant touch!

Kiesha

Jeremy

©1990 The Education Center, Inc.

9

Pop-up Invitations

Send these clever invitations to your Open House. Parents will find a surprise inside! The directions may sound complicated at first, but with the teacher demonstrating, even first graders can handle this project with great success.

Materials Needed: 9" x 12" construction paper, scissors, crayons or markers

Directions:

1. Hold paper vertically. Fold in half, left to right. Make a crisp crease.
2. Fold the paper in half again, this time from top to bottom. Make a crisp crease; then open the paper as it was in step one.
3. Along the folded edge, make a one-inch cut about two to three inches down from the center crease.
4. Fold back the cut edges to form two triangles. Be sure all creases are crisp.
5. Open paper fully; then refold into a card shape. The pop-up feature should open when the card is opened, but you may need to gently pry the paper up the first time it is used.
6. Draw a creature inside the card to fit the pop-up mouth or eye, and write a greeting.

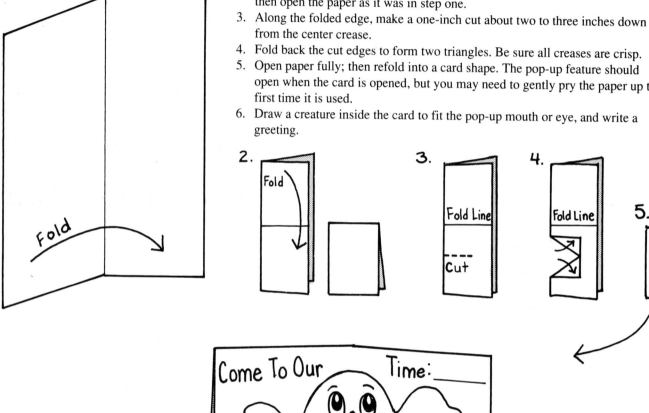

©1990 The Education Center, Inc.

Bits Of Americana

For a fun, group art project, create an American flag with bits of red, white, and blue. Tell students to look for blue jean–denim and ketchup-red pictures in glossy magazines at home. Have students cut or tear the colored paper into little bits about the size of their thumbs. Students can bring their bits of red and blue to school in Ziploc bags.

Provide a piece of white bulletin board paper (5' x 7') on which the field of blue and the red-and-white stripes have been outlined. Allow students to glue their bits of colored paper on the flag outline, overlapping the pieces. The class can work on this project in groups of four, during free time, over a period of two or three weeks. Let students add 50 white, cut-out stars to the field of denim-blue. Everyone will be proud of their contribution to this star-spangled display!

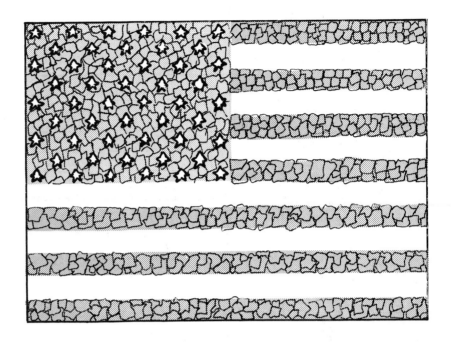

Window Painting

What do you get when you mix a window painting and sunlight? A spectacular display! Mix one-half cup liquid starch into one cup brown tempera paint. Paint a large tree trunk and branches on a classroom window. Children create tissue paper leaves and red apples to complete the September scene. Make these seasonal changes and keep your window decorated the entire school year: fall—iron crayon shavings between waxed paper and cut into leaf shapes; winter—add snowflakes cut from white paper; spring—add tissue paper leaves and colorful, spring flowers.

©1990 The Education Center, Inc.

A Wreath For All Seasons

To their delight, even first graders can make this lovely fall wreath. For each student you will need a tagboard ring (6 1/2" in diameter), eight yellow paper leaves and eight smaller orange leaves (patterns on page 14), a 12" length of yellow ribbon, a sprig of baby's breath, scissors, and glue.

To make each wreath, instruct students to position the tagboard rings on the tabletops in front of them. Imagining that each ring is a clock face, have each student glue a yellow leaf at 12 o'clock, 6 o'clock, 3 o'clock, and 9 o'clock. Then have students glue the four remaining yellow leaves in the empty spaces. Instruct students to glue each orange leaf so that it overlaps the edges of two yellow leaves. A yellow bow and a touch of baby's breath complete the effect.

Adapt this idea to have your students create wreaths of hearts in February and wreaths of tulip blooms in the spring.

Autumn's Harvest

Your students will enjoy "canning" fruits and vegetables and displaying their wares. For each student, duplicate a jar-shaped outline on white construction paper. Children fill their jars with fruits and vegetables by printing with various objects and paint colors. For example, a round block dipped in orange paint produces "peaches." A small round block dipped in red paint produces "cherries." When dry, attach printed labels. Cut out jars and display on a light-colored background with brown strips of paper representing shelves.

©1990 The Education Center, Inc.

Fall Foliage

Students can create a dramatic fall foliage display using construction paper and paint. Using the patterns on page 14, duplicate leaf patterns on yellow, orange, brown, and red construction paper. Cut out several leaves, crinkle them up, and soak them in water. Press each leaf flat on a protected desktop before dropping or painting irregular splotches of red, brown, orange, and yellow tempera paint on it. Crinkle the leaf in the palm of your hand again. Press each leaf flat on a protected surface and allow to dry. Display these leaves as embellishments or borders on classroom bulletin boards or attach them to sheets of black construction paper for eye-catching displays.

Chalk Shadows

Interesting chalk creations are lurking in the shadows! Cut a simple pattern from tagboard (leaf, heart, flower, kite, plane, balloon) and lay it on a 9" x 12" piece of white construction paper. Stroke colored chalk over the pattern while holding it in place. Move the pattern and repeat this process several times. Be sure to overlap the pattern and use an assortment of colored chalks. Spray the completed picture with hairspray to prevent smearing. Completed projects create a mystifying display!

Sandpaper Printing

Enjoy an easy project that's perfect for fall. Have each student use bright crayons to draw a picture on fine sandpaper; then place the sandpaper upside down on lightweight paper. Press with an electric iron set on medium until the crayon shows through the back of the paper. Because of the sandpaper's texture, the new picture will look as if it has been painted with hundreds of dots.

©1990 The Education Center, Inc.

Use with ideas on pages 12, 13, 19, 20, and 91.

©1990 The Education Center, Inc.

A Crop Of Corn

Harvest a bumper crop of Indian corn with this tissue paper activity. Wad brown, orange, yellow, and black squares of tissue, and glue them onto a tagboard, cob-shaped cutout to resemble Indian corn. Then staple beige or brown paper husks to the ears. If desired, place these bright ears of corn end to end for a harvest bulletin board border.

Wampum Necklaces

During a unit on Native Americans, make "wampum" necklaces by stringing Fruit Loops cereal onto strands of yarn. Tape one end of the yarn to keep it from unraveling during the process.

Rub A Note

Although leaf rubbings are always popular this time of year, you can use this "old favorite" technique to create newfangled notecards. Fold a sheet of paper in half twice as shown. Flatten the paper out, and designate two of the resulting sections as the areas for rubbings. Place a leaf, vein side up, beneath the sheet of paper. Rub the paper with the side of an unwrapped crayon. Repeat this procedure, overlapping the rubbings and using different leaves and different colors. Refold the paper to create a notecard. You may want to keep a supply of students' notecards on hand to be used as thank-you notes or greeting cards, or just to add a special touch to any communication.

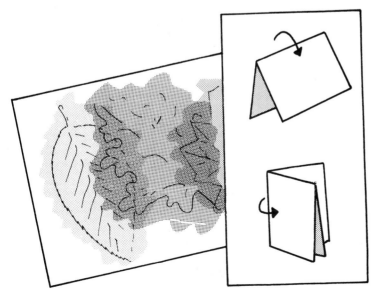

©1990 The Education Center, Inc.

Fall Mobiles

Take students on a fall nature walk to collect leaves, seeds, seed-pods, bark, and dried flowers to make classroom mobiles. Ask them to clean and save plastic pop bottles. Show students how to mount each natural object between two pieces of cold laminating film or clear Con-Tact paper. Then have them cut around each object, leaving an edge of film. Use an X-acto knife to cut off the top of a two-liter, plastic pop bottle for the top of each mobile. Punch holes in it and in each laminated object using a paper punch. Tie yarn through the holes to hang the various objects. Hang mobiles in the classroom where students can examine them.

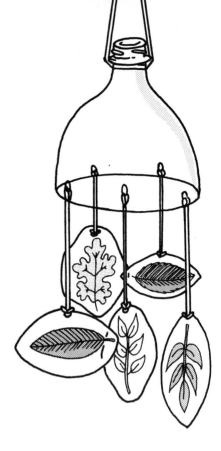

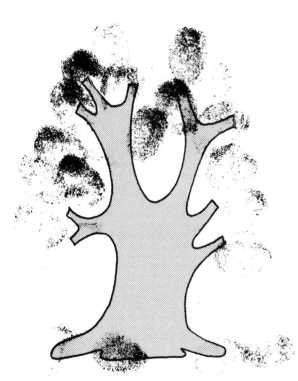

Fingerprint Trees

Fingerprints are not a nuisance—they're a necessity for this art project. On art paper, duplicate page 17. Color the tree trunk; then put one teaspoon of finger paint near the top of the tree. Repeatedly dip a finger into the paint and onto the branches of the tree until the branches are covered with fingerprint leaves. Scatter a few "leaves" below the tree too. For color-mixing fun, substitute small dollops of yellow and red for the teaspoon of paint. The colors will overlap and intermingle, creating the look of fall foliage.

Crumpled Art

Your students can achieve unique results with this crumpled paper technique. Cut the front and back panels from brown paper grocery bags. You will need one panel per student. Have each student crumple his paper over and over again, then flatten it out. Dunk the paper in a pan of water until it is thoroughly soaked. Hold the paper over the pan until the excess water has dripped off. Provide colored chalk for drawing on the paper. Hang these projects up to dry. If desired, mount on construction paper or cut into simple shapes before displaying.

16

©1990 The Education Center, Inc.

Pattern

Use with "Fingerprint Trees" on page 16,
"Autumn-matic Art" on page 19, and
"Watercolor Autumn Leaves" on page 21.

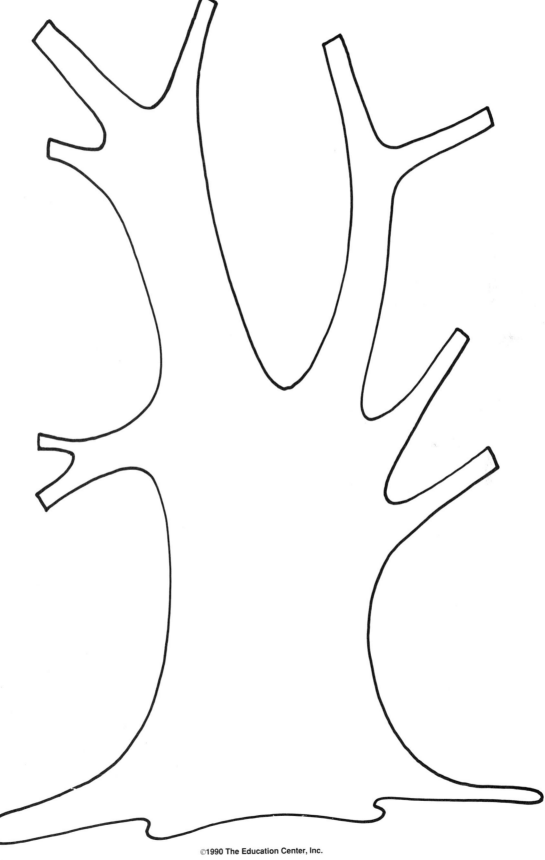

©1990 The Education Center, Inc.

All things are beautiful...

in time.

Leafy Print

Here's a creative autumn leaves project. Brush acrylic paint on leaves; then arrange them, paint side up, on a newspaper-protected surface. Place a small piece of white fabric (8" x 8" is an easy size to handle) on the leaves and press. Lift carefully and let dry. Students can complete their leaf prints by writing original poems on the fabric with fine-point markers.

Leaf Lanterns

Try this variation on leaf pressing that will produce colorful leaf lanterns.

Materials: fall leaves, waxed paper, iron, 4" x 16" strips of orange construction paper, 2" x 12" strip of brown construction paper

Directions:

Give each student two pieces of waxed paper 15" long. Have the student arrange leaves between the waxed paper sheets. Press with a hot iron. Staple orange strips to the top and bottom of the waxed paper. Roll and staple to form a cylinder. To make a handle, staple a brown paper strip to the cylinder. To turn the lantern into a basket for collecting leaves, staple a plastic bag inside the cylinder.

©1990 The Education Center, Inc.

"Autumn-matic" Art

Add more dimension to your autumn art projects using paper plates as the background. Paint a thin paper plate blue using watercolor paint. Begin with a tan (or gold), construction paper half-circle to match the diameter of the paper plate. Trim the half-circle; then glue to the rim of the paper plate to represent the foreground as shown. Next glue a brown, construction paper tree cutout (pattern on page 17) to the foreground. Glue small bits of red, yellow, orange, and brown construction paper or tissue paper to the tree and foreground for leaves. Then attach a yellow circular cutout (sun) and white cotton balls (clouds) to the background. Add cutouts of people engaged in typical fall activities such as playing football, or add cutouts of typical fall sights such as baskets of apples or garden harvests. Staple yarn to the back of the paper plate and tie in a bow for a hanger. These projects will "autumn-matically" be a hit with your students.

Striped Pictures

Combine brightly colored stripes and cutouts for an unusual fall art project. Each child uses a pencil and ruler to cover a piece of white paper with lines going in different directions. After coloring between the lines, the child adds three to five cut-out leaves (see patterns on page 14). Encourage children to place their leaves in interesting designs.

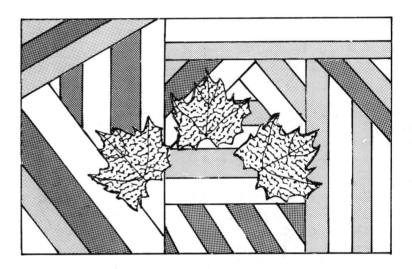

Native American Art

Native Americans recorded important tribal events by painting symbols on animal skins. Your youngsters can simulate this type of communication using brown paper bags, paint and/or potato prints. Select Native American symbols from a reference book to share with your youngsters. Repeatedly wad up a large piece of brown paper bag which has been torn to resemble an animal skin. Then spread the paper out on a flat surface. Using bright colors of paint such as red, yellow, and orange, paint or potato print the symbols of your choice onto the paper. These imitation animal skins make a striking and intriguing display to complement your Native American studies.

©1990 The Education Center, Inc.

Fall Leaves Banner

Children will enjoy making banners to celebrate the fall season. Let students cut many sizes and styles of leaf shapes from materials as varied as tissue paper, foil, wrapping paper, felt, doilies, finger paintings, etc. (See the leaf patterns on page 14.) For a three-dimensional look, fold the paper leaves and crumple the tissue and foil ones. Cut an old sheet or piece of burlap for the banner, bind its bottom edge or add fringe, and glue leaves to the material. At the top add a dowel and string for hanging. Make other monthly banners with colorful pumpkins, tree ornaments, snowflakes, hearts, shamrocks, and flowers!

Tissue Paper Leaves

Brighten your classroom with cheery, stained-glass pictures. Have each student paint a 9" x 12" piece of white tissue paper with watercolors in fall shades. Be careful not to get the tissue too wet or it will tear. While the tissue dries, let each child trace and cut out leaf shapes from a 9" x 12" piece of black construction paper, leaving at least 1/2" around the edge. (See the leaf patterns on page 14.) Glue the tissue to the back of the black paper. Tape the finished artwork to a window, and let the sun shine through!

©1990 The Education Center, Inc.

Watercolor Autumn Leaves

These leaves look like the real thing! Have each child cut out 12 leaves from yellow or orange construction paper. The child can curl the ends up slightly by wrapping leaves around a pencil. Next, children stroke various shades of pastel watercolors across the leaves to give the appearance of turning. Students cut tree trunks from brown paper (pattern on page 17) and glue each trunk to a 12" x 18" piece of red paper. They arrange and glue leaves on and around the trees. Mount the trees on a wall for a splash of fall color!

Colorful Fall Leaf Mobile

Duplicate an oval frame and fall leaf pattern on colored construction paper. You will need two copies of the same color for each child. The student cuts out his two oval frames and two leaves. He glues one oval frame and one leaf on top of a folded piece of waxed paper as shown. Next he adds crayon shavings between the waxed paper. Cover with plain newsprint, and press with a warm iron so the crayon melts. Trim the excess waxed paper. The child turns the project over so the waxed paper side is up. He then places the other oval frame on the waxed paper to match. To finish, the child inserts a piece of yarn with the second leaf attached, and glues the frames together. Punch a hole at the top for hanging.

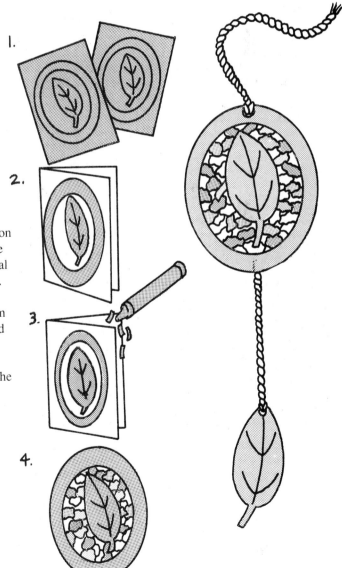

1.

2.

3.

4.

Pumpkin Decoration

For a colorful fall display, try these translucent pumpkins. Draw a pumpkin on a piece of white paper. Lay a sheet of clear plastic wrap over the drawing. Squeeze white school glue along the lines. Press black yarn onto the outline and let dry. Mix a little glue and green food coloring in a paper cup. Use a thick coat of this mixture to paint in the stem area. Repeat this procedure using a thick coat of orange glue for the pumpkin. Let the pumpkin dry for one day. Peel the decoration from the plastic and hang from a light fixture with a length of yarn. This technique can be used for holiday wreaths, Valentine's Day hearts, and spring butterflies and flowers.

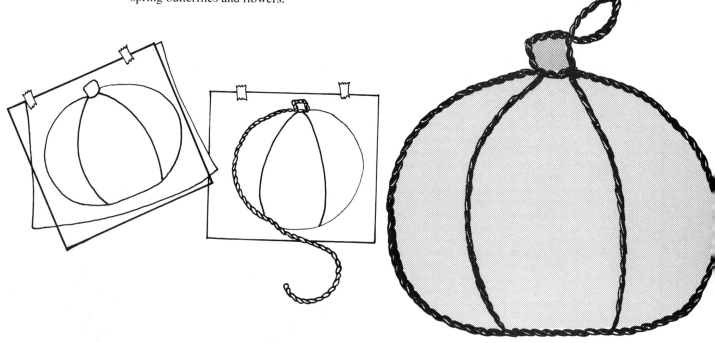

Autumn Hoot Owls

Fill your room with a flock of fall owls. Fold a piece of 12" x 12" brown construction paper as shown. Glue two 3" yellow circles onto two 3 1/4" black circles for eyes. Glue to the owl. Fold a 2" x 2" orange square in half, diagonally, and attach to the owl for the beak. To finish, fringe the bottom edge of the owl to "ruffle his feathers."

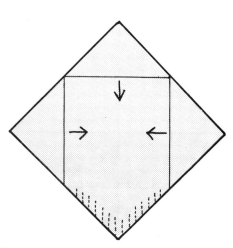

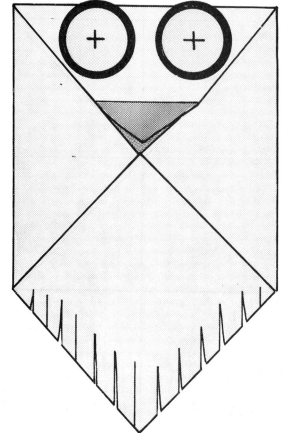

22   ©1990 The Education Center, Inc.

Halloween Treat Bags

Send students home ready for Halloween with a fun art project. Glue wiggle eyes to a large, black pom-pom (one per child). Instruct each student to glue his pom-pom to a small orange or brown bag. Have the child use a black marker to add eight, furry spider legs and a Halloween message. Before heading home, students can fill their bags with party treats (stickers, pencils, candy, etc.).

Coat-Hanger Characters

Transform coat hangers into floating jack-o'-lanterns and galloping ghosts! To make each character, bend a coat hanger into the desired shape. Apply a coating of white glue around the hanger; then place the hanger, with the hook extending, between two sheets of tissue paper. Pat the layers together. After the glue dries thoroughly, trim any excess paper. Add construction paper features and green tissue stems. Hang these spooky characters from your ceiling.

Halloween Silhouettes

Create a stunning Halloween silhouette in a few easy steps. Begin with a 10" x 16" piece of yellow construction paper. Streak a sponge dipped in orange tempera paint across the paper from left to right until the entire paper is streaked. After the paint dries, glue two 16" x 1/2" black construction paper strips across the bottom of the page, and add several three-inch strips vertically to make a fence. Add a black cat and a white moon. Mount the picture on a 12" x 18" piece of black or orange construction paper.

©1990 The Education Center, Inc.

glue to back of cat

Halloween Cat Mobile

To make a Halloween mobile, duplicate the cat pattern on page 25 on black paper. After cutting out the cat, cut a black circle slightly larger than the cat's width. Start at the edge and cut in a circular manner to the center. Glue to the base of the cat. Use colorful stickers and paper strips for the eyes, collar, nose, and whiskers. Hang from the ceiling.

Silhouette Pictures

Use a silhouette effect to make spectral Halloween scenes! Paste construction paper figures on white paper with rubber cement. Spray with dark paint; then remove the figures and rubber cement. Colored pencil details and contrasting paper frames add the finishing touches!

Ghost-Go-Rounds

Capture your students' imaginations with these ghosts which can be worn as necklaces. Have each student place three cotton balls in the center of an eight-inch-diameter circle of thin, white cloth. Using yarn, tie this area off for the ghost's head. Place single cotton balls opposite each other on the fabric. Tie them off using a single, 15-inch strand of yarn, and let the haunting begin!

cotton balls

finished project

©1990 The Education Center, Inc.

Pattern

Use with "Halloween
Cat Mobile" on page 24.

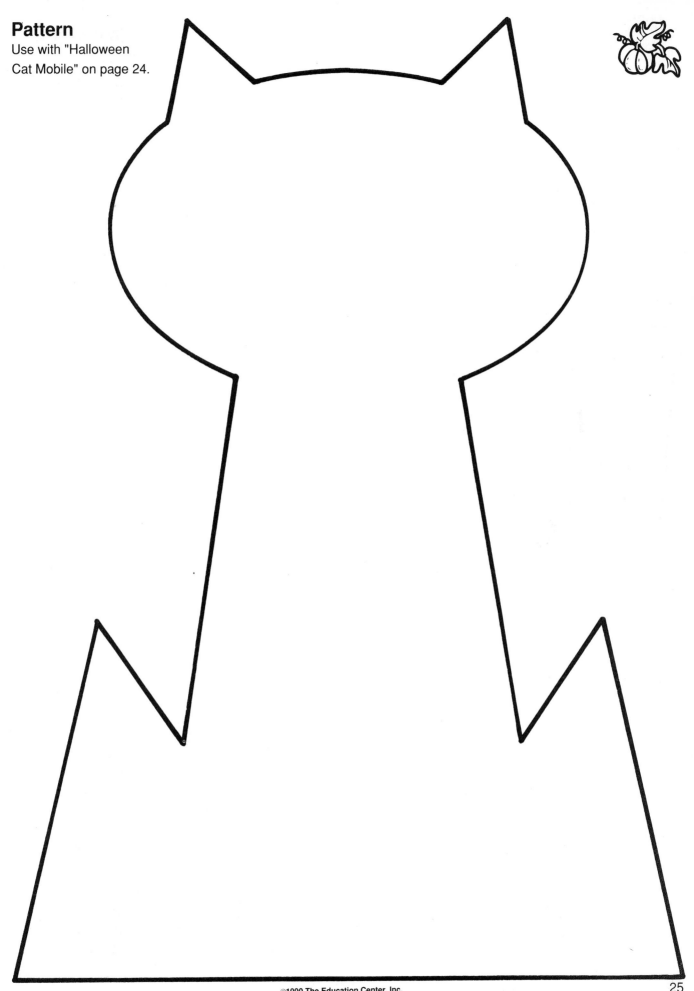

©1990 The Education Center, Inc.

25

Apple-Head Witch

Here's a Halloween project that students will remember for years. With parents' help at home, each child peels an apple and cuts slits in the "face" shown. The apple is then placed on a Popsicle stick or pencil and brought school. Students use the following materials and steps to complete their apple-head witches:

Materials needed for each student:

two black-eyed peas (or other dried beans)	white polyester filling
uncooked, white rice	12-inch square of black fabric
black pipe cleaner	black construction paper
glue	stick
yarn scraps	scissors

Directions:

1. Place peas in slits for eyes. Stick grains of rice in mouth for teeth.
2. Let apple dry for several days. Watch witch's head turn darker and shrin Use your fingernails to add a wrinkled brow or to make a chin.
3. Glue polyester filling on head for hair.
4. Cut a slit in center of fabric square and slip it on the stick.
5. Use the pipe cleaner to secure fabric to stick or pencil and to make witc arms.
6. Make witch's hat from black construction paper. Glue to head.
7. Use a stick and yarn scraps to make a broomstick. Place it in your witch pipe cleaner arms!

Two-faced Jack-o'-Lanterns

To make these hanging pumpkins, paint the bottoms of two paper plates orange. Add black-line details when dry if desired. Cut a happy face in one plate and a sad face in the other. Glue black paper behind each plate. Add a green paper stem and curly vines before gluing the plates together. Hang from the ceiling with yarn.

©1990 The Education Center, Inc.

Great Ghosts!

Holes from your hole puncher make great, dazzling ghosts! Each child uses a toothpick to glue the dots to black construction paper to make a ghost. Students glue cut-out eyes to small strips of paper, folded accordion-style, and glue them to their ghosts for a 3-D effect. Use glitter to "dress up" the eyes. Punch black holes to form spiders, bats, and other spooky creatures. Or use orange punches to make Halloween jack-o'-lanterns!

Paper Sack Haunted Houses

Have children construct haunted houses with spooky residents. Begin by having students decorate white paper sacks to look like haunted houses. Help children glue the bottoms of the bags to decorated cardboard and stuff with newspaper. After adding construction paper roofs, students add cut-out witches, ghosts, vampires, and other creepy inhabitants!

Illuminating Art

This cut-out window art project is sure to lure everyone's attention!

Materials: dark bulletin board paper (enough to cover your classroom window), art knives, orange tissue paper, tape, board

Directions:
1. Place a board under the bulletin board paper.
2. Have students cut Halloween designs (scary faces, etc.) in the paper with art knives.
3. When designs are completed, tape the tissue paper behind them.
4. Tape the paper to a window, and enjoy the frightfully fun display!

©1990 The Education Center, Inc.

Centerpiece Show-off

Perk up your room with student-made centerpieces just in time for Open House. Cut, or have students cut, construction paper circles the same diameter as the doilies you'll use for this project. Glue each doily to a paper circle. (If doilies are not available, glue one construction paper circle to another, smaller, paper circle of a contrasting color.) Glue bright, colorful leaves around the construction paper circle. Top these creations with small student-decorated jack-o'-lanterns, gourds, a vase (plastic cup) of wildflowers, or the black cats described in "Black Cat Surprise" (page 29). These cheery decorations are sure to set an upbeat atmosphere for your Open House guests.

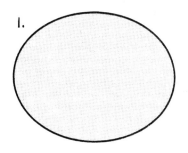

Bright-eyed Jack-o'-Lanterns

Set the scene for Halloween with these watchful jack-o'-lanterns. Cut large pumpkin shapes from 9" x 12" pieces of orange construction paper. Next cut the pumpkin shapes, as shown, into one-inch strips. Place the strips in order on 12" x 16" pieces of black construction paper. Glue the strips down, leaving small spaces between the strips. Cut jack-o'-lantern faces from yellow construction paper. Glue the features onto black construction paper and cut out again, leaving a black trim. Glue jack-o'-lantern features onto pumpkins. Add stems made from green construction paper.

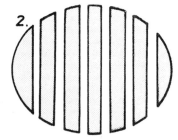

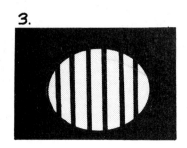

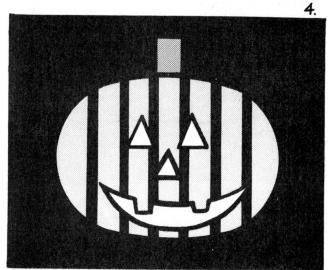

©1990 The Education Center, Inc.

Spooky Carbon Crayon Resist

Here's a fun art project that requires used duplicating carbons. Distribute used carbons and white sheets of paper to students. Have each student place the white paper atop the carbon (carbon side up) and draw a Halloween design. Throw out the carbons and turn the papers over. Have students color their designs with crayons. When finished, have students hold their artwork under running water. The carbon will wash over the picture, creating a resist effect. (Be sure to have rubber gloves available to keep ink off hands!) Let drawings dry; then display them in your classroom.

The Pumpkin Patch

Create a patch full of pumpkins! Students stuff lunch bags with newspapers and twist the tops. Help children secure pumpkin tops with masking tape. Each student paints his stuffed bag orange. When the pumpkins are dry, the children create faces by gluing black construction paper shapes in place. Finish the pumpkins by using green construction paper to cover the masking tape and adding curly green ribbons for vines.

Black Cat Surprise

This Halloween kitty is "purr-fectly" willing to sit up and pay attention in your October classroom. Trace the patterns (page 30) on black construction paper and cut out. Fold the larger pattern as shown. Glue on yellow construction paper or sequins for eyes, or attach wiggle eyes. Glue six 1 1/2-inch pieces of thin spaghetti or pipe cleaners for the whiskers. When dry, lift the cat's head and glue only the top portion of the cat's legs to his body. Be sure to have the cat's legs extending just a little below his body. Set the kitty on a tabletop or windowsill among pumpkins or jack-o'-lanterns for an air of Halloween mystery.

fold

©1990 The Education Center, Inc.

29

Patterns
Use with "Black Cat Surprise" on page 29.

©1990 The Education Center, Inc.

Halloween Owls

For a Halloween creature that can hold lots of treats, remove the top from a milk carton. Spiral a band of crepe paper from bottom to top, pasting only the upper edge of the band. Gently stretch the unpasted edge to create a 3-D, feathery effect. Add paper features and a yarn handle for carrying.

Jaunty Jack-o'-Lanterns

Follow these directions for jack-o'-lantern faces that peek from inside orange pumpkins.

1. Cut a rectangle and eight strips of paper twice as long as the width of the rectangle.
2. Decorate the rectangle with a jack-o'-lantern face.
3. Glue side edges to form a cylinder.
4. Glue ends of each strip inside the cylinder at the top and bottom edges.
5. Add a green or brown paper stem.

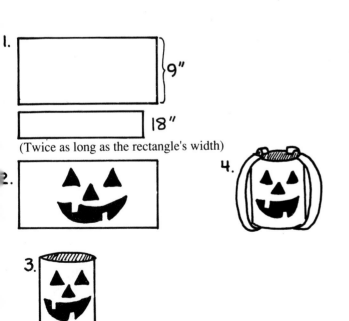

©1990 The Education Center, Inc.

Dancing Spiders

Your students will enjoy entertaining their friends with this spider craft.

Materials:
small squares of black tissue paper
scissors
tape
small, shallow box (without lid)
acetate sheet, slightly larger than
 top of box
black marker

Directions:
1. Draw one side of a spider on a folded piece of tissue. Cut out spider. Bend the legs as shown to make them jointed. Make several more spiders like the first one.
2. Draw a web on the inside bottom of the box.
3. Place your spiders in the box. Tape the acetate sheet over the of the box.
4. Rub the acetate and watch the spiders jump! The rubbing creates static electricity, which makes the spiders jump.

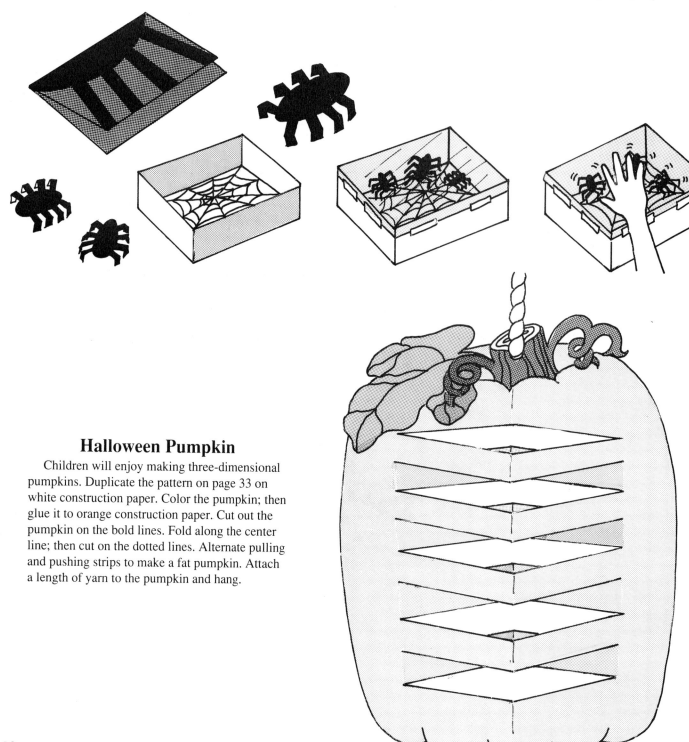

Halloween Pumpkin

Children will enjoy making three-dimensional pumpkins. Duplicate the pattern on page 33 on white construction paper. Color the pumpkin; then glue it to orange construction paper. Cut out the pumpkin on the bold lines. Fold along the center line; then cut on the dotted lines. Alternate pulling and pushing strips to make a fat pumpkin. Attach a length of yarn to the pumpkin and hang.

©1990 The Education Center, Inc.

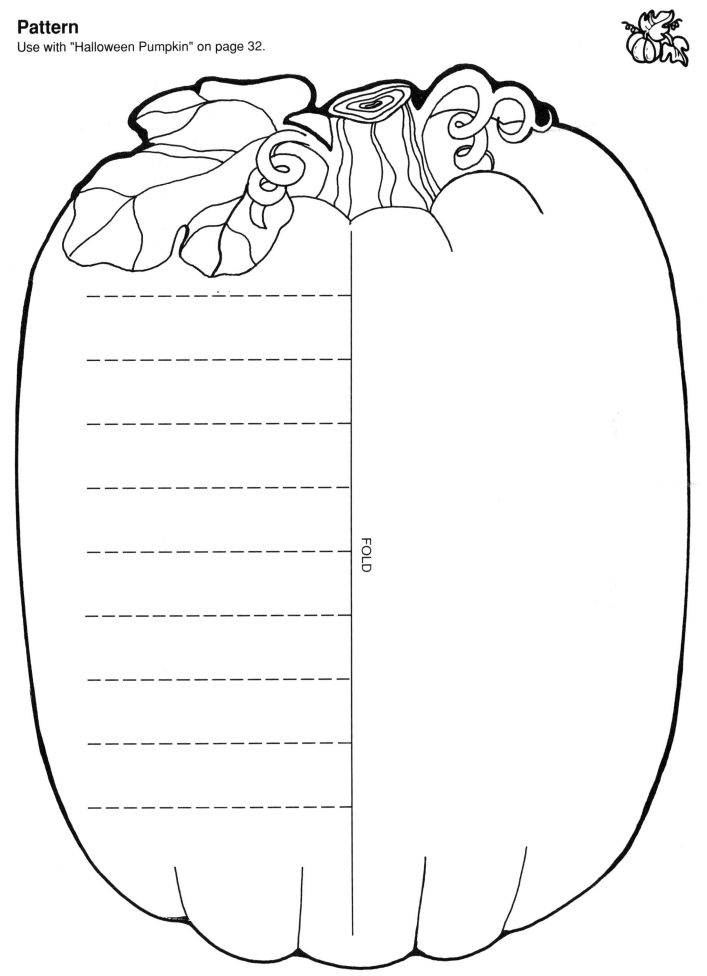

FOLD

©1990 The Education Center, Inc.

"Boo-tiful" Pencil Toppers

Delight your youngsters by having them create friendly spooks to give as gifts or to add a seasonal touch to their own pencils. Cut two ghosts from white felt. With a fabric marker, add eyes and a mouth to one cutout. Then glue or stitch the two ghost cutouts together, leaving an opening at the bottom. When the glue is dry, slide the ghost atop a pencil. This little ghost just might motivate youngsters to do "boo-tiful" work!

Mask Masquerade

Your students won't be able to mask their joy when they've created these out-of-the-ordinary Halloween mask. For each student, cut eyes from an oval Chinet plate. Usin masking tape, attach a paint stirrer to each plate. Then lay strips of newsprint dipped in papier-mâché paste on the back of the plate to create facial features. When the featur are formed as desired, top with strips of colored tissue paper which have been dipped in watered-down glue. For dazzling sheen, spray the mask with varnish. Organize a Halloween parade so students can masquerade behind the original mask designs.

Harvest Centerpieces

Every Thanksgiving the table needs a centerpiece, which your students can make in a snap. Head outdoors on a crisp, autumn day to collect greenery, leaves, and other outdoor materials. Have students donate small pumpkins (squashes, gourds, and apples will also work). Each child uses a nail to poke holes in his pumpkin. Greenery and leaves are then inserted to make an attractive centerpiece.

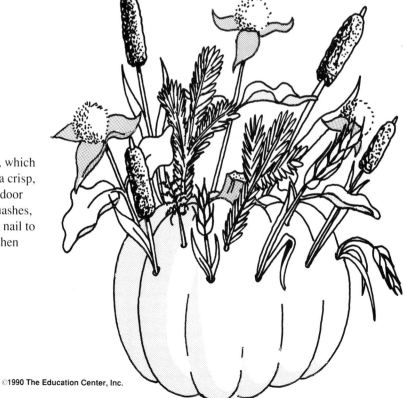

©1990 The Education Center, Inc.

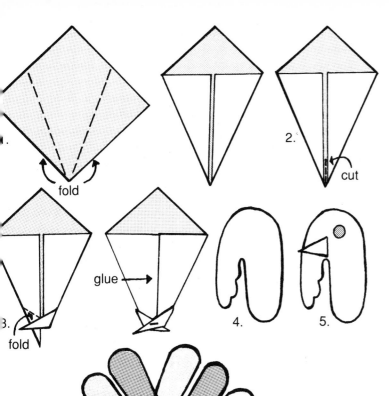

fold

2.

cut

glue →

3.
fold

4.   5.

6.

Folded-Paper Turkey

Stuff these paper turkeys for Thanksgiving party favors.

Materials: scissors, crayons, stapler, glue, and construction paper—a 12" x 12" brown piece for the body, a 2 1/2" x 7" red piece for the head, a yellow piece, and six colored pieces for the feathers

Directions:
1. Fold the 12" x 12" piece of paper as shown.
2. Cut on the center fold line two to three inches up.
3. Fold right leg. Fold left leg. Staple right leg over left leg. Glue two flaps of body together where indicated.
4. Cut out a red turkey's head.
5. Cut a triangular beak from yellow construction paper. Paste the beak on the head. Add an eye and glue head onto body.
6. Cut and paste feathers onto body.
7. Fill turkey with popcorn, peanuts, or raisins.

Tissue Turkeys

Brighten up your classroom for the holiday season with these colorful turkeys. Duplicate student copies of the turkey pattern on page 36. Have students color, cut out, and mount the turkeys on white construction paper. Next instruct students to draw in tail sections as shown. Students wrap brightly colored tissue paper squares around their pencil erasers and glue these tissue paper twists closely together on the tail sections of their turkeys.

©1990 The Education Center, Inc.

Pattern
Use with "Tissue Turkeys" on page 35, "Crayon Shaving Turkeys" on page 37, and "Handprint Turkey" on page 41.

36

©1990 The Education Center, Inc.

Giant Turkey

Fall leaf colors make this gobbler special! Have students place leaves between sheets of newsprint. Put several heavy books on top of the newsprint to press the leaves flat. Have students use the pressed autumn leaves to make a giant turkey's tail on a bulletin board. After lightly sketching the head, body, and feet onto the bulletin board background paper, have several students color the body brown; then let children work in small groups to glue seeds, mosaic-fashion, onto the turkey's head and feet. Gently pin or glue the leaves to the body as the turkey's tail feathers.

Crayon Shaving Turkey

Cut a turkey body from brown paper (see pattern on page 36) and place on a sheet of waxed paper. Sprinkle crayon shavings where the feathers would be. Cover with another sheet of waxed paper and iron. Attach black construction paper strips to the top and bottom, punch holes in the top, and hang with yarn.

Blow Art Turkeys

Have each student paint a turkey (without feathers) onto white paper, then add drops of tempera or watercolor paint around the body's edges. The child then uses a straw to blow the paint drops to produce an unusual, feathered effect.

©1990 The Education Center, Inc.

Napkin Rings

Holiday napkin rings will make Thanksgiving dinner a special treat! Cut 6" x 2" felt strips; then overlap ends and glue. Cover the seams by pasting on paper cutouts of various Thanksgiving symbols (see patterns below). Use markers to add color to the cutouts.

Patterns

©1990 The Education Center, Inc.

Turkey Fans

Fancy fans create feathered turkey centerpieces! Fold three, identical, rectangular pieces of brown construction paper like fans, keeping folds neat and even. Connect the three folded papers with clear tape as shown. Pull both ends together, forming a straight edge. Fasten securely with tape. Cut out a turkey head, color both sides, and tape to the middle of the turkey feathers.

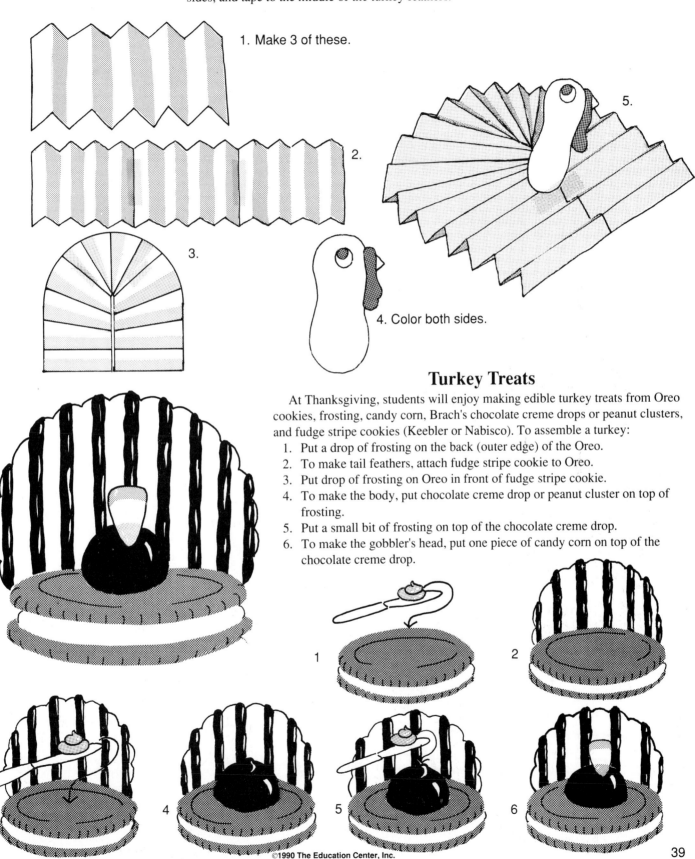

1. Make 3 of these.

2.

3.

4. Color both sides.

5.

Turkey Treats

At Thanksgiving, students will enjoy making edible turkey treats from Oreo cookies, frosting, candy corn, Brach's chocolate creme drops or peanut clusters, and fudge stripe cookies (Keebler or Nabisco). To assemble a turkey:

1. Put a drop of frosting on the back (outer edge) of the Oreo.
2. To make tail feathers, attach fudge stripe cookie to Oreo.
3. Put drop of frosting on Oreo in front of fudge stripe cookie.
4. To make the body, put chocolate creme drop or peanut cluster on top of frosting.
5. Put a small bit of frosting on top of the chocolate creme drop.
6. To make the gobbler's head, put one piece of candy corn on top of the chocolate creme drop.

1

2

3

4

5

6

©1990 The Education Center, Inc.

Potato Turkeys

Send your students home for Thanksgiving break with creative centerpieces! Insert toothpicks and gumdrop halves into a medium potato to make the turkey's legs and feet. Duplicate the patterns below on white construction paper for each child. Color and cut out the patterns. Make a vertical cut in the potato and insert the head. Cut slits between the tail feathers on the dotted lines and attach to the potato with toothpicks or glue. Attach wings in the same manner.

Patterns

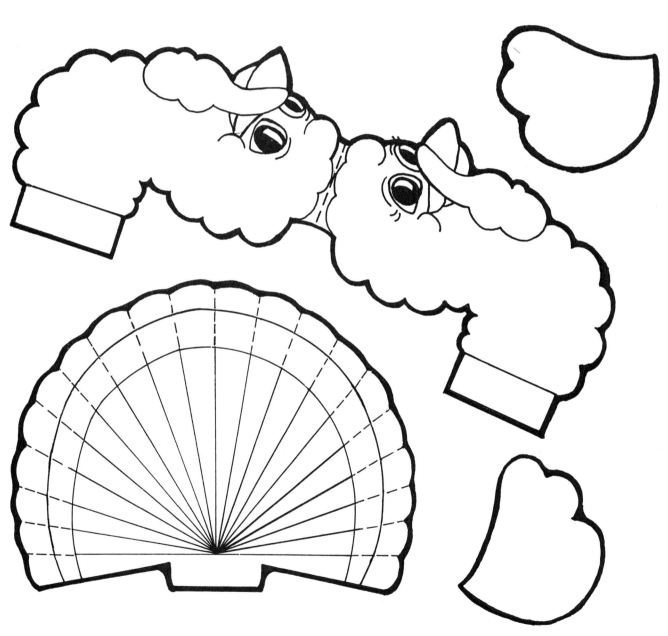

©1990 The Education Center, Inc.

Handprint Turkey

For a quick afternoon art project, work with your students to make a Thanksgiving bulletin board. Trace, color, and cut out a turkey (pattern on page 36), and mount it on a bulletin board. Have students trace their hands on multicolored construction paper, cut them out, and staple to the board for feathers. Your group effort will produce festive results!

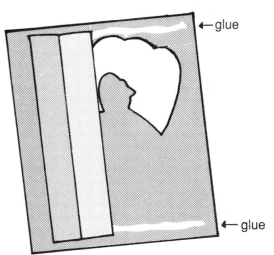

← glue

← glue

"Technicolor" Turkey

Your students will be proud as peacocks of these turkeys. Duplicate the pattern (on page 42) on brown construction paper for each student. Cut on the dotted lines and cut a variety of colors of tissue paper into 1" x 10" strips. On the back of the construction paper, run thin lines of glue above and below the cut-out section. Press tissue paper strips into place, overlapping slightly. Use markers or crayons to color the turkeys' beaks, wattles, and feet.

©1990 The Education Center, Inc.

Pattern

Use with " 'Technicolor' Turkey" on page 41.

42

©1990 The Education Center, Inc.

Winter

Colorful Holiday Greetings

Spread the holiday spirit with these colorful greetings. In large block letters, have each student write a holiday word. Using red and green crayons, students color and decorate each letter uniquely. Including an occasional sprig of holly and a bow adds to the effect. To complete the project, students cut around the letters and glue the words to red or green sheets of construction paper.

Holly And Holiday Candles

Bring the warm glow of Christmas into your classroom with these cheerful candles. Have each student paint a bathroom tissue tube red. When dry, spray the tube with adhesive and sprinkle on clear glitter. Add construction paper or tissue paper flames. Place each student's candle in a holly ring before displaying on the windowsill.

Styrofoam Printing

Here is an activity to introduce your students to the art of printing. First have them save Styrofoam meat trays.

Give each student a meat tray on which to draw a picture with a dull pencil. Pour a little tempera paint into an aluminum pan. With a brush or roller, each student covers his picture with paint. Take a piece of construction paper, folded in half, and press it against the painted meat tray. Turn it over for a few seconds. Flip the tray back over and carefully remove the paper. The picture will be printed on it. Repeat the above process to make as many prints as desired. This makes wonderful stationery and invitations, as well as holiday greeting cards.

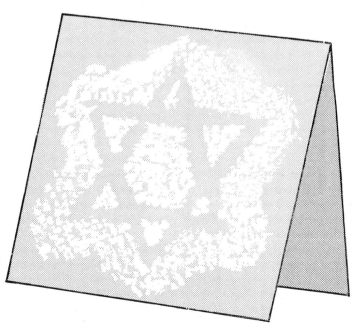

Hole-punched Christmas Trees

Have fun making different sizes of hole-punched Christmas trees. Display on windows, and let the sun light up the trees.

Materials: 1/2 sheets of 9" x 12" black construction paper, scissors, small pieces of assorted colors of tissue paper, hole punchers, glue, glitter, yellow construction paper

Procedure:

1. Fold black paper in half lengthwise. Cut along open edge to resemble one side of a Christmas tree.
2. Leave paper tree folded in half and punch numerous holes all over tree.
3. Unfold tree. On one side, glue assorted colors of tissue paper over holes.
4. Turn tree over. Finish decorating by using glue and glitter to make scallops of garland. Add a yellow, construction paper star.

Mini Sleighs

These mini sleighs will make attractive party favors for your class. Cut a section from a pressed cardboard egg carton and shape it to look like the body of an old sleigh. Paint the cup red and glue on pipe cleaner runners. Add several pieces of wrapped candy among holly leaves.

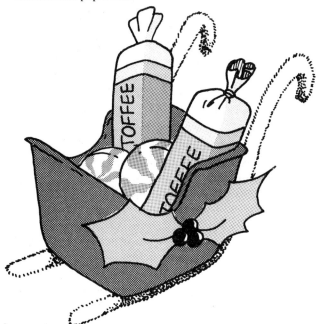

Pretzel Wreath

Here's a gift for Mom and Dad that looks good enough to eat! Glue five small pretzels together in a circle. Glue on a second layer of pretzels overlapping the first and spray with shellac. Weave in ribbon, tie with a bow, and attach a hanger. Cut a tagboard circle a little larger than the inside of the wreath and cover with metallic paper. Glue a child's photo on the cut-out circle; then glue behind the wreath. Makes a nice ornament too!

©1990 The Education Center, Inc.

Hanging Holiday Decorations

These three-dimensional decorations can be strung from the ceiling to give your room a holiday atmosphere. Duplicate the patterns below on heavy paper. (For larger decorations, enlarge the patterns before duplicating.) Trace and cut out five identical shapes from construction paper. Layer the five cutouts, staple in the center of all five thicknesses, and fan out the layers. Next trace and cut out ten of the same shape, but one-third the size of the first cutouts. Fold these slightly and glue into the "pages" of the larger shapes. Contrasting colors give a festive effect. Add string or yarn for hanging.

Patterns

©1990 The Education Center, Inc.

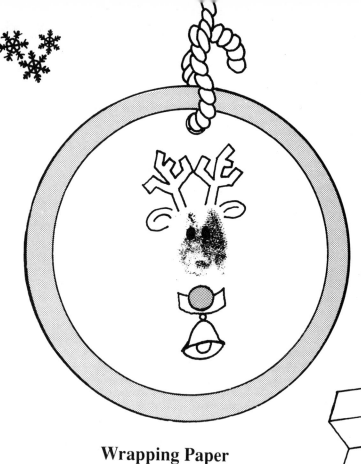

Keepsake Ornaments

These Christmas ornaments are inexpensive and make cu[...]
keepsakes.

How to make:
1. Spray paint a small jar lid inside and out.
2. On white paper, draw a circle slightly larger than the l[...]
3. Press a red or green thumbprint in the circle; then draw[...]
   features to make a person or animal. Personalize the
   ornament with your name and the date.
4. Laminate and cut out the circle.
5. Push the circle into the lid.
6. Punch a small hole in the lid and insert yarn for
   hanging.

Wrapping Paper

Here is a simple way to make colorful and unique wrapping
paper for Hanukkah and Christmas gifts. First fold a sheet of
white tissue paper, accordion-style, to a width of two inches.
Beginning at one end of the folded paper, fold as you would a
flag, making triangles with each fold. After the last fold, you
will have one thick triangle. Dip each corner in water and then in
different colors of food coloring. Allow to dry overnight, since
the paper tears easily when wet. Unfold. Each sheet will be
colorful, different, and ready to use!

Step 1

Step 2

Step 3

Step 4

Step 5

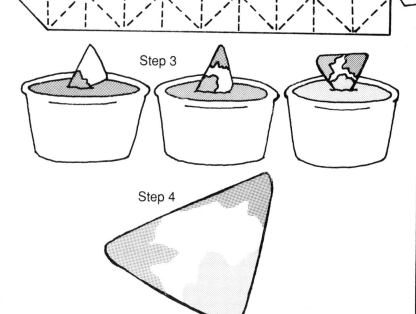

©1990 The Education Center, Inc.

Light Bulb Ornaments

Turn old, burned-out light bulbs into colorful tree ornaments. Have children bring in old bulbs over the year so you will have a variety of shapes and sizes by Christmas. Make a batch of papier-mâché paste. Give each child a bulb and newspaper strips. (Place bulbs in egg cartons so they won't roll.) Have children alternate applying layers of paste and paper. Be sure each child attaches a yarn loop for hanging while applying paper to his ornament. Let the ornaments dry in the egg cartons; then have students paint them with bright colors of tempera.

"Hand-some" Tree

Everyone can lend a hand to help with this display. Have students trace the outline of each of their hands onto three shades of green construction paper and cut out. Starting at the top, work your way down the tree, stapling one additional hand cutout in each row. After the greenery is in place, add a brown paper trunk and student-made ornaments. Now that's a "hand-some" tree!

Rudolph Ornament

Rudolph, with his nose so bright, will add a touch of whimsy to any Christmas tree. For each Rudolph you'll need a pinecone; one nine-inch, white pipe cleaner; white and black felt; glue; and a small, red pom-pom. Fold the pipe cleaner in half, bend like stairs into antlers, and glue onto the pinecone. Cut the felt into circles; then glue on the pinecone for eyes. Finish by gluing on the pom-pom nose and a length of yarn for hanging.

©1990 The Education Center, Inc.

Make A Christmas Village

Let everyone lend a hand to construct a festive Christmas village! Trace or duplicate the pattern on heavy paper. Use markers or crayons to decorate the pattern with store signs, windows, fancy doors, etc. Cut on the solid lines; then fold on the dotted lines and paste together. To make a warehouse or church, add 1/2" at the bottom of the pattern. For a one-story house, subtract one inch from the bottom.

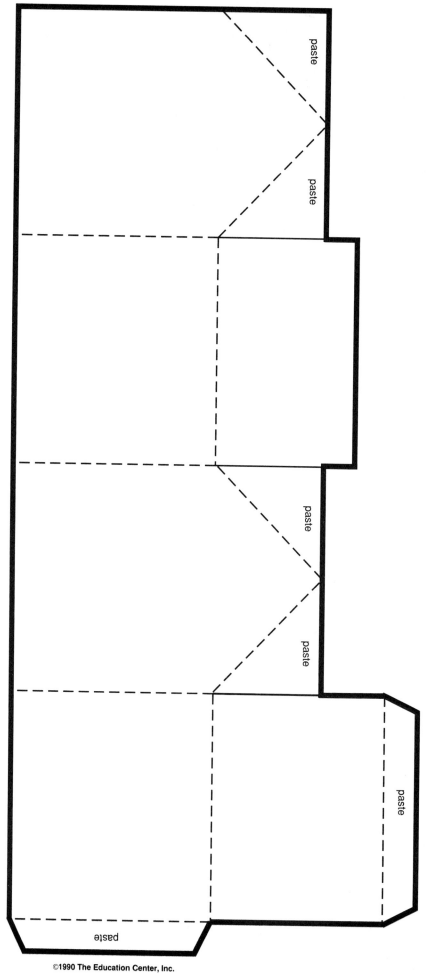

paste

paste

paste

paste

paste

paste

©1990 The Education Center, Inc.

Christmas Craft Day

Instead of a Christmas program, invite parents to come to the classroom and make "gingerbread houses" with their children. Before the Craft Day, ask each child to bring in one type of candy to decorate the houses. Also ask the custodian to save small milk cartons from the cafeteria. Wash the cartons; then staple each one shut. On Craft Day, mix the candies and place a bowlful on each table. To make the houses, "glue" graham cracker walls to the sides of the milk cartons using royal icing (see recipe). Attach the candy to the walls using the icing as well. The royal icing will harden within an hour so children can take their houses home to use as holiday centerpieces. To add to the festive time, play Christmas music and serve punch and cookies. What a special way to celebrate Christmas together!

Royal Icing

For every four students, mix 1 cup confectioner's sugar, 1/4 teaspoon cream of tartar, and 1 egg white. Using caution, stir in 1/3 cup boiling water. Beat at high speed for 10 minutes.

Paper Menorahs

Combine measuring skills and drawing to create these important symbols of Hanukkah. To make a menorah, use 9" x 12" construction paper, a ruler, a pencil, scissors, and markers.

Steps:

1. Measure and mark the 12-inch side of the sheet into thirds. Draw lines across the sheet.
2. On the top third of the sheet, measure and mark each inch along the 9-inch side. Draw lines so that this part is divided into nine equal rectangles.
3. Measure and mark one inch from the top and one inch from the bottom of this section. Draw lines across the sheet.
4. Draw a candle inside each rectangle. The shammash, the extra helping candle, should extend beyond the other candles (see diagram). Color the candles' flames.
5. Carefully cut around the candles.
6. Bottom third of sheet: Fold the bottom edge of the paper up to the drawn line and crease. Fold up again at the drawn line and crease. Write a Hanukkah message on this part as shown. This third of the sheet can now stand in tentlike fashion.
7. To complete the project, fold down the top third of the sheet (the candles) so that it will stand.

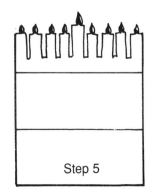

Steps 6 and 7

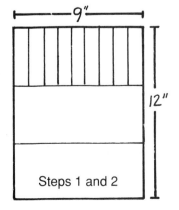

Steps 1 and 2

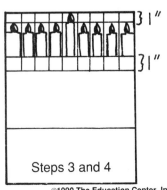

Steps 3 and 4

Step 5

©1990 The Education Center, Inc.

Punched Tin Ornaments

These old-fashioned, punched tin ornaments can be made quickly and easily. They look especially beautiful when placed directly in front of a Christmas tree light.

Materials needed include: hammers, small (not short) nails, lids from orange juice cans (the type with the plastic pull tab and no sharp edges), lace, glue, markers, and yarn.

Begin by drawing a simple design on the top side of the lid. Then punch evenly spaced holes on the design using a hammer and nail. Glue lace around the front edge. Add a piece of yarn on the back for hanging the ornament.

Santa Pencils

Here's a Christmas gift idea for your students that will make them say "Ho, Ho, Ho!" Attach red felt and quilt batting to a Styrofoam ball for Santa's hat and beard. Draw on a face using fine-tipped markers. Then make a hole for a pencil in the Styrofoam and glue the pencil in.

Festive Wreaths

Spruce up your classroom for the holidays with tissue paper wreaths. Cut out the center of a paper plate. Wrap a one-inch tissue paper square around the eraser end of a pencil, dip it into glue, and then press it onto the paper plate rim. When the rim is entirely covered with "greenery," glue on several small red circles (made using a hole puncher and red construction paper) for berries. Add a paper bow as a cheery finishing touch.

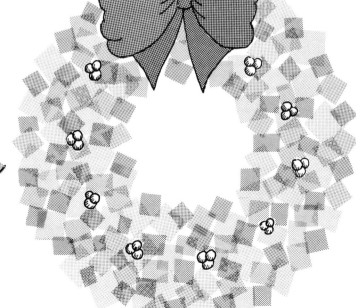

50

©1990 The Education Center, Inc.

Ice Cream Cone Ornaments

Turn your tree into an ice cream tree! Shellac a sugared ice cream cone. After drying, put glue around the inside edge of the cone and place a Styrofoam ball inside. When dry, cover the top of the ball and the top edge of the cone with glue and smooth on a circle (6 1/2" in diameter) of fabric, making small tucks around the edge. Tie a ribbon around the cone, pulling snugly. Loop 8" of ribbon, glue the ends together, and pin to the top of the ornament with a straight pin. Let the ornament dry completely before hanging.

Noel Hanger

A Christmas message hanging on the door welcomes visitors and makes a perfect gift for parents. To prepare for this project, have students cut out the felt bells ahead of time. Ribbons may be machine-sewn earlier too.

Materials needed for each student:
four green felt bells
one 18"–19" piece of 1 1/2" wide red ribbon (no. 9 ribbon of sealed-edge acetate works well)
one plastic curtain ring
white craft glue
gold glitter
scissors

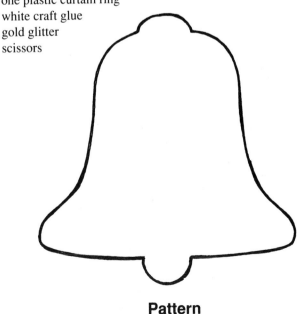

Pattern

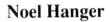

Directions:
1. Trace and cut out four felt bells using the pattern given or a cookie cutter.
2. Pull one to two inches of one end of the ribbon through the curtain ring. Secure by sewing through both pieces of ribbon.
3. Space and glue felt bells to ribbon. (A thin line of glue down the center works best.)
4. Outline one letter on each bell with glue to spell N-O-E-L. Sprinkle with glitter. Pour off excess glitter and trim any extra ribbon.

©1990 The Education Center, Inc.

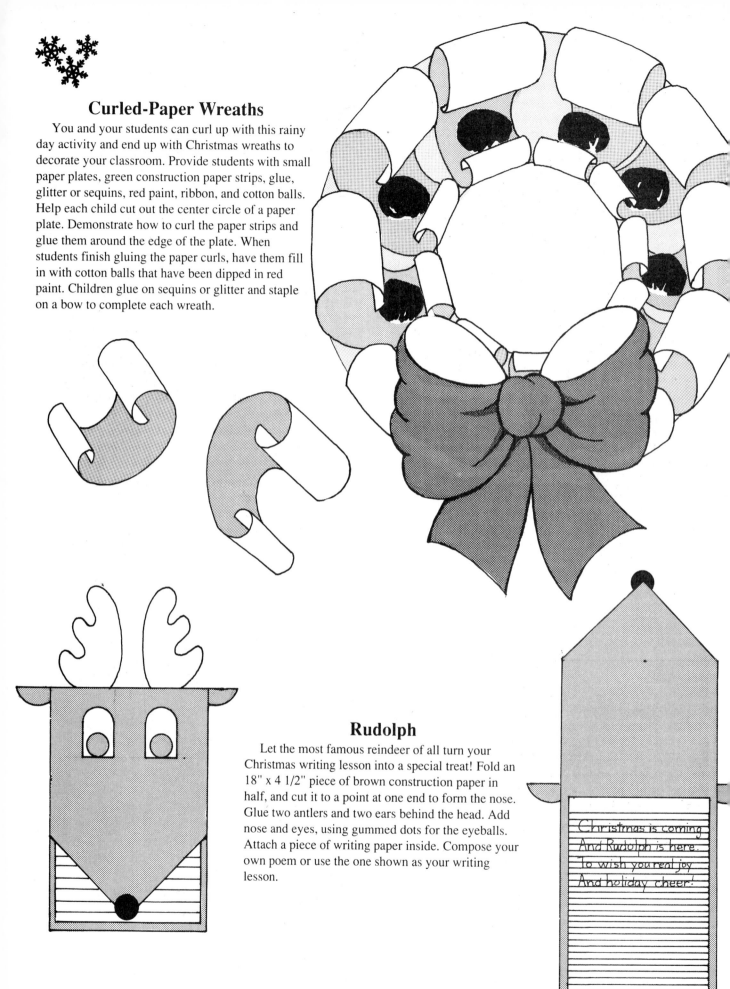

Curled-Paper Wreaths

You and your students can curl up with this rainy day activity and end up with Christmas wreaths to decorate your classroom. Provide students with small paper plates, green construction paper strips, glue, glitter or sequins, red paint, ribbon, and cotton balls. Help each child cut out the center circle of a paper plate. Demonstrate how to curl the paper strips and glue them around the edge of the plate. When students finish gluing the paper curls, have them fill in with cotton balls that have been dipped in red paint. Children glue on sequins or glitter and staple on a bow to complete each wreath.

Rudolph

Let the most famous reindeer of all turn your Christmas writing lesson into a special treat! Fold an 18" x 4 1/2" piece of brown construction paper in half, and cut it to a point at one end to form the nose. Glue two antlers and two ears behind the head. Add nose and eyes, using gummed dots for the eyeballs. Attach a piece of writing paper inside. Compose your own poem or use the one shown as your writing lesson.

Christmas is coming
And Rudolph is here.
To wish you real joy
And holiday cheer!

52

©1990 The Education Center, Inc.

Silver And Gold Forest

Create the illusion of twinkling Christmas trees using metallic crayons. In advance, have your students donate silver, gold, and copper crayons. Make tree-shaped tagboard cutouts using the patterns on page 55. Cut black bulletin board paper into 8" x 10" sheets (one per student). Place a tree-shaped cutout beneath a sheet of black paper and rub the paper with a metallic crayon. Move the cutout to another location beneath the paper and rub again. Repeat until the page is filled with overlapping tree designs. Add decorations to each tree using contrasting metallic crayons.

Hanukkah Necklaces

Bake these Hanukkah necklaces during the holiday season so everyone can wear one with pride! Mix 1 cup salt, 3 cups flour, and 1/2 cup warm water. Add a few drops of blue or yellow food coloring. Knead until smooth. Roll as you would cookie dough. Let children use cookie cutters to cut out Star of David shapes. Poke a straw into each cutout before baking to make a hole for hanging. Bake at 250 degrees for about 30 minutes or until hard. Have children paint their stars and spray them with acrylic spray. When dry, have each student thread a piece of yarn through his star and tie it around his neck. Hanukkah necklaces may be given to parents or special friends during the holiday season.

Razzle-Dazzle Ornaments

For a dazzling ornament that's fun to make, place a piece of waxed paper over a Christmas pattern. Trace the outline of the pattern with glue. Immediately sprinkle the glue with glitter and let dry overnight. When dry, gently peel the waxed paper away from the shape and add metallic thread for hanging. Students can add extra touches by dotting more glue on top of a dried shape and sprinkling with another color of glitter.

©1990 The Education Center, Inc.

Christmas Carolers

Freestanding choir members make a festive holiday tabletop (or windowsill) display. One glance at these carolers and there's no doubt you'll be hearing the cheerful sounds of Christmas music.

For each choir member you will need:
tagboard duplicate of the face and hand patterns on page 55
12" x 18" sheet of red construction paper
4" x 12" piece of red construction paper
4" x 5" piece of black construction paper
5" x 8" piece of white construction paper
scissors
glue
stapler
tape
glitter pen (optional)

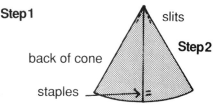

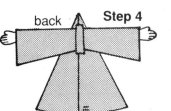

Directions for assembly:

1. **For the singer's body**, trim the large red rectangle as shown.
2. Bend the resulting half-circle into a cone shape and staple in place. Snip one-inch slits on opposite sides of the cone top as shown.
3. **For arms**, fold and trim the small red rectangle as shown.
4. Glue a hand cutout to each arm; then tape arms to the cone seam as shown.
5. **For songbook**, fold the black rectangle and tape to the palm of each hand as shown.
6. **For collar**, fold and cut the white rectangle as shown. Unfold and cut a triangular wedge from one side. Place the collar atop the cone.
7. Insert the face pattern. Fold under the triangular bit of the cone at the neck.
8. If desired, add glitter decorations to completed project.

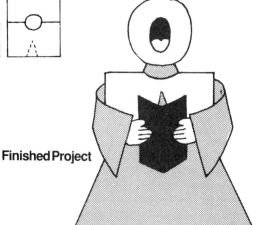

Dog Bone Christmas Ornament

Students will enjoy making Christmas tree ornaments from dog bone biscuits. To make the ornaments, you'll need dog biscuits, glue, wiggle eyes, small red pom-poms, red and black felt scraps, and red yarn. Use black felt for ears, and red felt for the tongue. Glue on wiggle eyes, pom-pom nose, and felt ears and tongue. Glue yarn on the back to hang.

©1990 The Education Center, Inc.

Use tree patterns with
"Silver And Gold Forest" on page 53.

©1990 The Education Center, Inc.

Seasonal Plates

Don't toss those disposable microwave plates—transform them! Draw and color a picture on a plate using permanent markers. Glue ribbon or lace around the plate rim using craft glue. For a hanger, tape an open paper clip to the back of the plate. Label and date the artwork using permanent marker. Voilà! A plate that was destined for the trash heap becomes a treasured family keepsake.

Giant Gingerbread Cookies

Students exercise their creativity as they convert finger-paint papers into gingerbread cookies. Enlarge the patterns on page 57 to make large cookies for students to trace. Have students trace the cookies onto their large, brown, finger-painted papers. Students then cut out and decorate to resemble decorated gingerbread cookies. Display these gingerbread cutouts on a bulletin board with the title "Run, Run, As Fast As You Can!"

Holiday Ornament

These appealing ornaments make nice presents for parents at Christmastime.

Materials: A potato chip can lid or any plastic lid with a lip; pinecones; dried beans or peas, or seeds; glue; thin ribbon; paper punch; student picture
Procedure: Punch a hole in the top of the lid. Carefully glue the student's picture in the center. Fill in the rest of the space by gluing down beans, peas, seeds, or pieces of cone. Thread a strip of ribbon through the hole for hanging. Be sure to allow plenty of drying time.

©1990 The Education Center, Inc.

©1990 The Education Center, Inc.

Santa Mobile

Decorate your room with a sackful of Santas.
Each student will need:
   two sheets of 9" x 12" red construction paper
   three sheets of 9" x 12" white construction paper
   cotton
   scissors
   thread
   glue

Follow these steps to make Santa mobiles to hang from your ceiling or window.

1. Cut out two identical hats and noses from red construction paper.
2. Cut out two identical beards and moustaches, and four identical eyebrows and eyes from white construction paper. Color the eyes on both sides.
3. Glue pieces of thread between the identical facial features as shown.
4. Glue the two beards together.
5. Tape the beard and threads with the facial features to one hat. Glue the other hat on top of it.
6. Glue cotton to both sides of the hat's tip, the hat's band, and Santa's beard.
7. Punch a hole in the top and hang with a piece of thread or yarn.

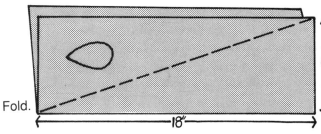

Fold.   —18"—   6"

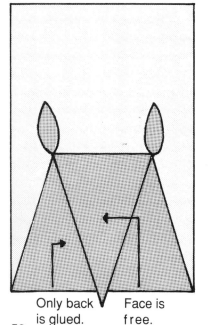

Only back   Face is
is glued.   free.

Holiday Reindeer

   These reindeer sport 3-D, Styrofoam antlers. Save peanut-shaped, Styrofoam packing pieces. Fold a 12" x 18" piece of brown construction paper in half. Cut on a diagonal line as shown. Save scraps for cutting ears. Position the unfolded brown triangle on blue paper, folding so that the tip of the triangle extends one inch below the background paper. Glue in place. Add ears and a shiny, red paper circle for a nose. Cut half-inch, black paper strips for eyelashes, and glue Rudolph. Add Styrofoam pieces for antlers. Cut and paste paper holly leaves for a collar.

©1990 The Education Center, Inc.

Personalized Holiday Ornaments

These large Christmas ornaments will add lots of sparkle and shine to your holiday room decor. Using a hole punch, punch holes around the rim of an aluminum tart pan. Use silver tinsel garland to stitch in and out of the holes in the pan rim. Tie off or tape the tinsel, and trim away the excess. Cut the center from a three-inch red construction paper circle. Use glue and glitter to add some sparkle to one side of the resulting ring. Tape a photograph behind the ring before gluing it to the bottom of the pan. For a hanger, thread ribbon, yarn, or a silver pipe cleaner through the uppermost hole in the pan rim. Students' smiles beaming forth from a classroom evergreen are certain to set your classroom aglow with holiday warmth.

Colored Chalk Greeting Cards

These colorful greeting cards are perfect for Hanukkah or Christmas. Cut a holiday shape pattern or use a cookie cutter. On a piece of folded construction paper, have each student trace around his pattern with a contrasting color of chalk. Keeping the pattern in place, have the student smudge the chalk by rubbing it with his finger. Remove the pattern, move it to another location on the paper, and repeat the tracing and smudging technique several times.

Angel Wings

Folded, paper lace doilies make pretty wings for these angel decorations. For shiny wings, apply glue to the inside of a folded doily. Insert a piece of gold or silver foil paper, and press layers together lightly. Glitter is optional. Glue wings to a white, Styrofoam cup. Glue on a Styrofoam ball head and yarn hair. Add facial features with markers. Attach a pipe cleaner halo.

©1990 The Education Center, Inc.

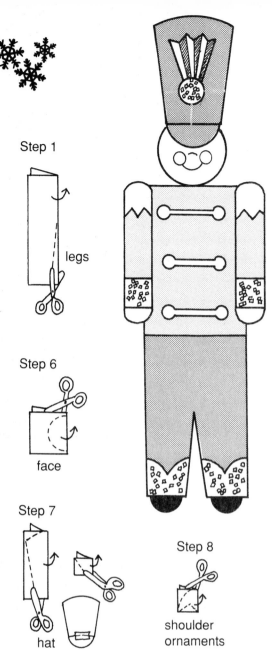

Step 1

legs

Step 6

face

Step 7

hat

Step 8

shoulder
ornaments

Toy Soldiers

For an eye-catching hallway or bulletin board display, position these prim
and proper soldiers shoulder to shoulder. Advance preparations are necessary
for this project, and students must listen carefully to the directions for
assembly. But the payoff for your efforts is big, bold, and beautiful!

Construction paper needed for each toy soldier:

7" x 12" piece of blue   a 2" tan circle
7" x 10" piece of red   a 3" black circle
(2) 2" x 9" pieces of red   (2) 1" pink circles
5" x 7" piece of tan
5" x 7" piece of black   **Additional supplies:**
2" x 5" piece of black   scissors, glue, tape
(2) 2" squares of yellow   a black marker
yellow, red, and green for decorations   glitter (optional)

Directions for assembly:

1. **For the soldier's legs,** fold the blue rectangle in half and trim near the
   fold as shown. Unfold.
2. **For feet,** cut the black circle in half. Glue each half to the bottom of one
   leg.
3. **For chest,** glue the large red rectangle to the legs cutout.
4. **For arms,** glue the small red rectangles to the sides of the chest.
5. **For hands,** cut the tan circle in half. Glue each half to the bottom of one
   arm.
6. **For face,** fold and cut the tan rectangle as shown. Unfold and glue it
   atop the chest. For cheeks, glue on the pink circles. Add a smile and
   nose with black marker.
7. **For hat and brim,** fold and trim the black rectangles as shown. Unfold
   cutouts. Tape the smaller cutout (brim) to the larger cutout (hat),
   allowing the paper to bow outward. Glue the hat atop the face.
8. **For shoulder ornaments,** fold and trim the yellow squares as shown
   and glue atop the arms.
9. Further decorate the soldier using yellow, red, and green paper, and
   glitter.

Graph Paper Art

Graph paper and cross-stitch designs make
colorful art projects. Duplicate the patterns on
the following page for students. Give each
student a sheet of graph paper and a pattern
page. The student selects a pattern and makes
X's in the graph paper squares using the
colors indicated. To create a Christmas
display, mount finished work on red and
green paper.

60   ©1990 The Education Center, Inc.

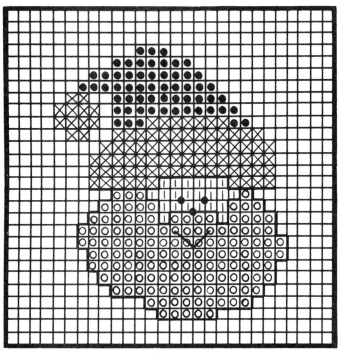

Santa

- • Red
- ○ White
- | Pink
- X Grey

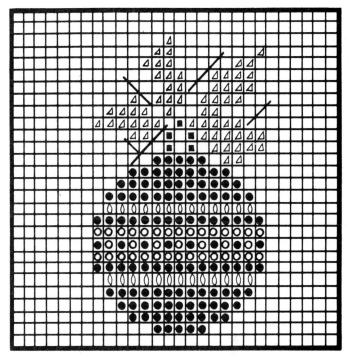

Ornament

- • Red
- ◖ Purple
- ○ Yellow
- ■ Black
- ◿ Green

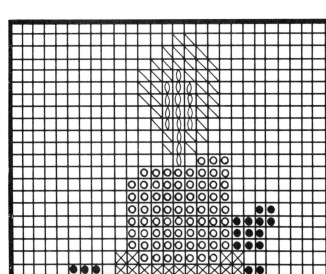

Candle

- ╲ Yellow
- ◖ Orange
- ○ Red
- • Green
- X Black

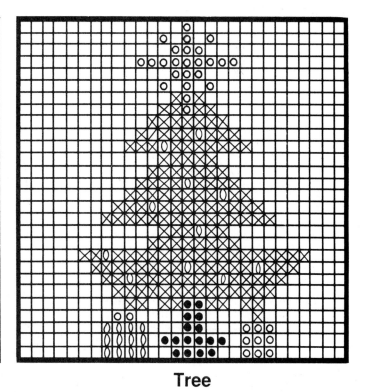

Tree

- ○ Yellow
- • Black
- X Green
- ◖ Red

©1990 The Education Center, Inc.

Giant Ornaments

Create a dazzling display of giant Christmas ornaments using your students' artwork. Begin by collecting oversized samples of student artwork. (Art paper must be at least 16 inches square.) Artwork may include finger-painted papers or chalk rubbings. Or have students drizzle glue randomly on art paper and paint (when dry) with watercolor paints. Another suitable technique is "marbleizing." Students place art paper on the surface of a pan of water that has been sprayed with two colors of enamel paint. Cut the selected samples into 16-inch circles.

For each student, duplicate a copy of the ornament top on page 63 on gray construction paper. Have students glue the ornament tops to their artwork. Suspend these giant ornaments on varying lengths of ribbon or yarn. Displayed together, they have marvelous impact outside your classroom door or on a large bulletin board.

Hanukkah Crinkled Creations

Looking for an unusual Hanukkah project? Crinkled, aluminum foil Stars of David will fit the bill. Have each student crinkle and flatten a piece of aluminum foil before cutting it into the shape of a Star of David. With a mixture of egg yolk, powdered detergent, and blue food coloring, have each student paint his cutout, leaving a bit of foil showing here and there. Allow for drying time. Have students glue the foil stars onto blue construction paper and trim to within 1/2 inch of the edge of the foil.

Salt Dough Photo Frames

Salt dough photo frames are another neat holiday gift for students to make for their parents. Mix two parts flour with o part salt. Add a little water slowly to achieve the same textur Play-Doh. Give each child enough dough to roll into a fat sn Turn the snake into a circle by joining its ends. Smooth the e together and insert a paper clip in the circle to use for hangin Let the frames dry for several days, or bake them in an oven 250 degrees for one hour. When the frames are completely d they can be painted or shellacked. Attach a small photograph the back of the frame.

62 ©1990 The Education Center, Inc.

©1990 The Education Center, Inc.

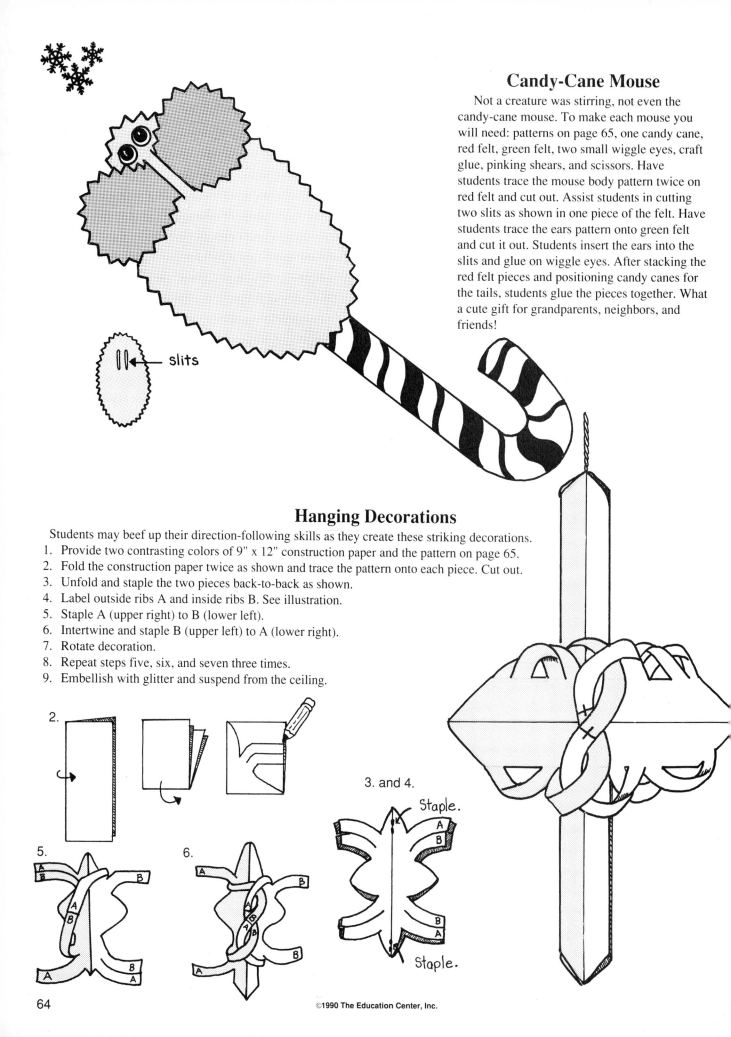

Candy-Cane Mouse

Not a creature was stirring, not even the candy-cane mouse. To make each mouse you will need: patterns on page 65, one candy cane, red felt, green felt, two small wiggle eyes, craft glue, pinking shears, and scissors. Have students trace the mouse body pattern twice on red felt and cut out. Assist students in cutting two slits as shown in one piece of the felt. Have students trace the ears pattern onto green felt and cut it out. Students insert the ears into the slits and glue on wiggle eyes. After stacking the red felt pieces and positioning candy canes for the tails, students glue the pieces together. What a cute gift for grandparents, neighbors, and friends!

← slits

Hanging Decorations

Students may beef up their direction-following skills as they create these striking decorations.
1. Provide two contrasting colors of 9" x 12" construction paper and the pattern on page 65.
2. Fold the construction paper twice as shown and trace the pattern onto each piece. Cut out.
3. Unfold and staple the two pieces back-to-back as shown.
4. Label outside ribs A and inside ribs B. See illustration.
5. Staple A (upper right) to B (lower left).
6. Intertwine and staple B (upper left) to A (lower right).
7. Rotate decoration.
8. Repeat steps five, six, and seven three times.
9. Embellish with glitter and suspend from the ceiling.

2.

5.

6.

3. and 4.

Staple.

Staple.

©1990 The Education Center, Inc.

Patterns

Use with "Candy-Cane Mouse" on page 64.

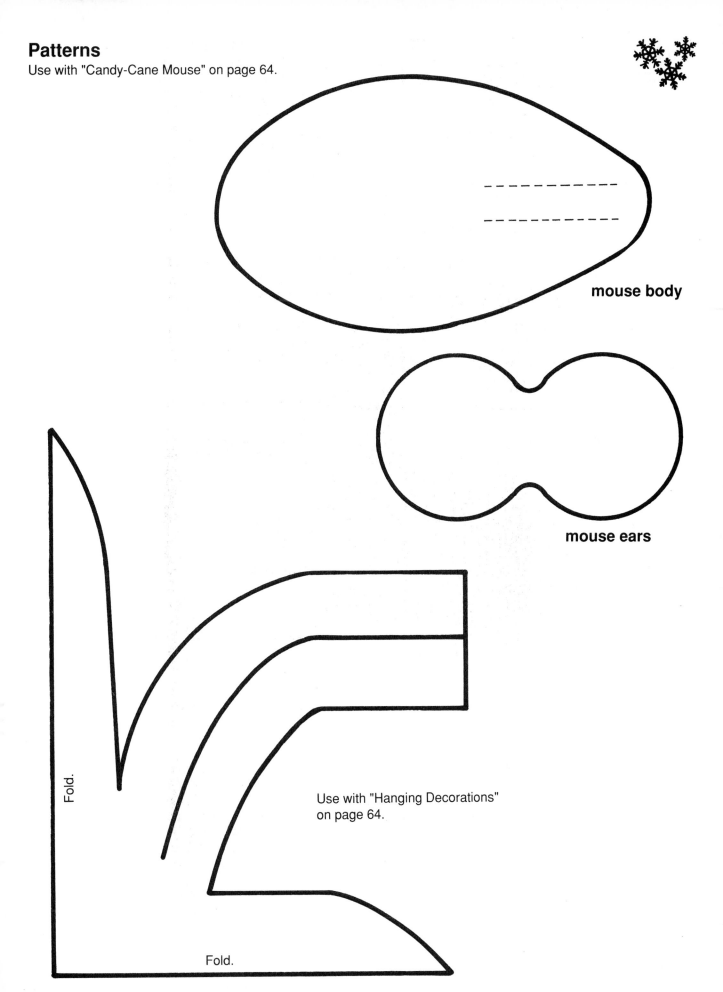

mouse body

mouse ears

Fold.

Use with "Hanging Decorations"
on page 64.

Fold.

©1990 The Education Center, Inc.

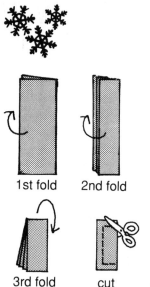

1st fold   2nd fold

3rd fold   cut

Snowflakes On Windowpanes

A blizzard of snowflakes obstructs the view from these waxed paper windowpanes. Fold several squares of white paper and cut to create snowflakes. Press the snowflakes between two sheets of waxed paper using a warm, protected iron. Fold a 9" x 12" sheet of black construction paper in half vertically; then fold vertically again, pressing the folds to flatten. Fold the paper once again—horizontally this time. Using scissors with a good cutting edge, trim away a rectangular area as shown. Unfold and flatten the paper. Staple it to the waxed paper–encased snowflake design, and trim away the excess waxed paper. Suspend these winter windowpanes from the ceiling or attach them to classroom windows.

Blizzards Are In The Forecast

When the local weather forecaster is calling for midwinter snowstorms, your youngsters will enjoy producing a blizzard or two of their own. Have students draw winter scenes on art paper and color thoroughly with crayon. Using large brushes and diluted, white, tempera paint, have students whitewash their papers to lend a snowy effect to the artwork. Bundle up. A blizzard's on the way!

Winter Wall Hanging

A winter wall hanging is a great follow-up activity for studies of the four seasons. Cut an old white sheet into 12" x 16" rectangles. Stretch a rectangle on each child's desk over a piece of drawing paper. Secure with masking tape. Using markers, have each student draw a seasonal picture. Then stitch the rectangles together into a wall hanging. Add a three-inch border of inexpensive fabric. A wall hanging is the perfect cover-up for an unsightly wall.

©1990 The Education Center, Inc.

Paper Flurries

Suspend a flurry of snowflakes from your classroom ceiling to create a delicate, wintry atmosphere. Duplicate the snowflake pattern onto tagboard and cut out. Have each student trace the pattern onto one white and one colored piece of folded paper as shown and cut out. After unfolding each cutout, instruct students to place one atop the other, refold twice as shown, and cut several shapes from the folded side of the cutouts. Have students unfold and staple on the original fold lines, and attach yarn for hanging. Students may add a bit of sparkle, if desired, by spraying the snowflake cutouts with aerosol adhesive and sprinkling on transparent glitter.

Pattern

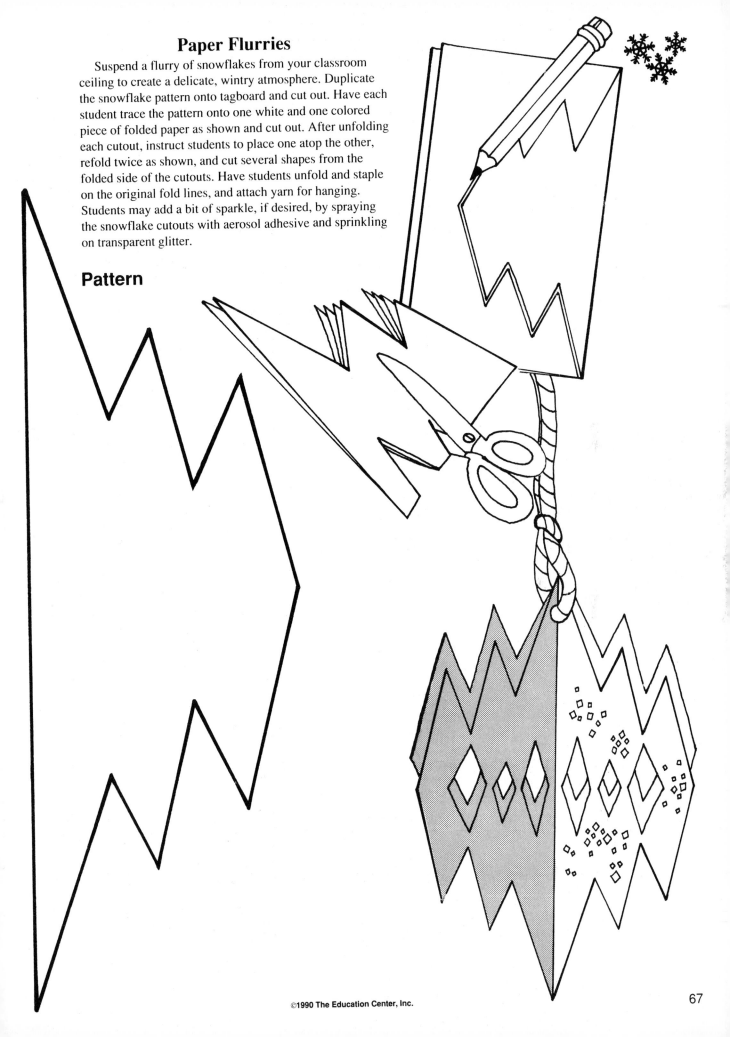

©1990 The Education Center, Inc.

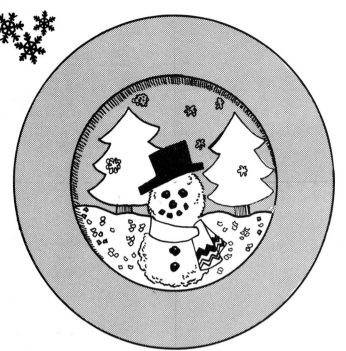

Tiny Snow Scene

Welcome winter with a fun paper plate project. Trace a paper plate two times on blue construction paper. Cut out the circles. Paste one circle on the plate; then cut the center out of the second circle and put aside. Create a snow scene by pasting a cotton ball snowman, snowflakes cut from doilies, shaved Styrofoam "snow," and construction paper details on the paper plate. Frame your scene with the blue paper ring cut out earlier.

Snow People

Fill your room with these smiling, little snow people. Use the pattern to make several oaktag snowmen. Give each child a 4 1/2" x 8 3/4" piece of white construction paper. Fold in half and then in half again so that a fold is on each side. Let children trace the oaktag pattern as shown (arms on folds), cut it out, and open it up. Students add clothes and features using paper or fabric scraps, crayons, and markers. Post side by side across the front of the room for a delightful winter display.

Pattern

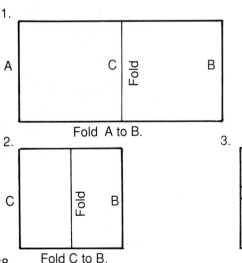

1.

A   C | Fold   B

Fold A to B.

2.

C | Fold   B

Fold C to B.

3.

Cut out.

68   ©1990 The Education Center, Inc.

Sparkle, Snowflake, Sparkle

Sparkle away those winter blahs with these glittering snowflakes. Have students fold and cut white paper to make snowflake designs. Next have each student place his unfolded snowflake on a square of clear Con-Tact covering and trim to within 1/4" of the perimeter of the paper. Encourage students to sprinkle glitter and/or white sequins over the snowflakes and tap off the particles which do not adhere to the Con-Tact covering. Whether you attach these glittering snowflakes to your classroom windows or winter bulletin boards, you're certain to get a little lift from the cheerful sparkles.

Snowfall Silhouettes

Simple, snowy silhouettes have wonderful impact when displayed together on a bulletin board. Provide a sheet of black construction paper, white art paper, and glue for each student. Have students tear white paper into various shapes to create winter scenes and glue the paper onto the black construction paper. Bits of paper glued to the background of the scene produce the illusion of flurries.

A Pasta Blizzard

When it's threatening to snow outside, have your students create a blizzard indoors using pasta. To make a pasta snowflake, roll one piece of wheel-shaped pasta in a pie plate containing white glue, and place it on a sheet of waxed paper. Then position additional pieces of pasta to encircle the first piece. Be certain that each of these pieces butts against the glue-covered pasta. One at a time, dip six more pasta wheels in glue and butt the glued portion of each between two previously glued pasta wheels. Squeeze a generous drop of glue on each of the exterior pasta wheels, opposite the center of the design. Place a shell- or spiral-shaped pasta in each glue drop, butting against the wheel-shaped pasta. When dry, peel the "snowflakes" from the waxed paper and spray paint them white. When the paint is dry, spray the snowflakes with adhesive spray and sprinkle on Twinklets Diamond Dust or clear glitter. Pin these glistening snowflakes to winter bulletin boards or suspend from the ceiling on monofilament line to create a classroom blizzard.

©1990 The Education Center, Inc.

Snowman Fashion

Use graph paper and three different-colored crayons or permanent markers to make paper snowman clothes. Color a sheet of one-inch-square graph paper, alternating colors. Draw mittens, buttons, a scarf, and a hat on the back of the sheet of graph paper after coloring; then cut out. Paste on a snowman drawing or cut-out snowman for an unusual suit!

Snowflake Art

Arouse your students' curiosity with the prediction of afternoon snow flurries! To begin, each student cuts nine snowflakes from tissue paper in variety of sizes and colors (pastels and blues work nicely). Students then arrange their tissue cutouts 11" x 17" pieces of white construction paper and glue in place. With paintbrushes and water, the students gently brush outward from snowflake centers to their points. This process helps adhere snowflake points and gives the project a blended look. Mount dry projects on 12" x 18" pieces of colored construction paper.

Plastic-wrapped Winter Scenes

Here's a new way to wrap up art for winter. Have children bring in white, Styrofoam meat trays. Provide simple, winter pictures from coloring books or magazines, and have each child choose a scene no larger than his tray. Students tape the scenes to their desks and tape plastic wrap over their pictures. Next each child traces the outline of his picture in black permanent marker. He fills in with other colors, leaving snow areas clear. When the coloring is completed, each student lifts the plastic wrap off his desk and places it over the flat side of the meat tray, taping edges under. The white tray makes a great snowy background. Display on a bulletin board with the title, "A Snowy Day."

©1990 The Education Center, Inc.

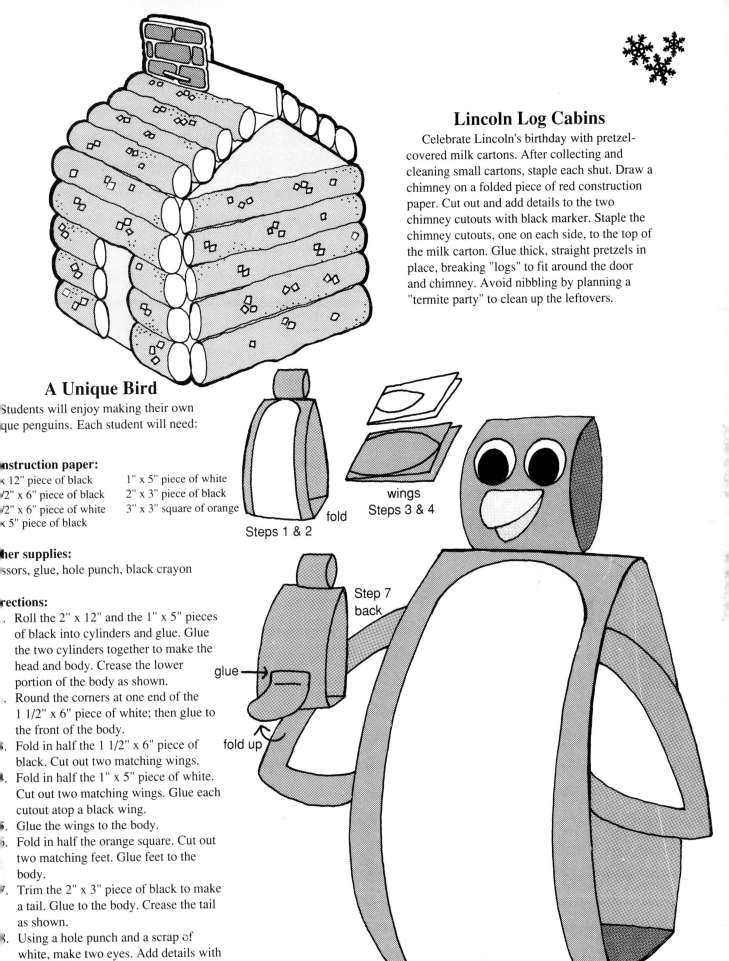

Lincoln Log Cabins

Celebrate Lincoln's birthday with pretzel-covered milk cartons. After collecting and cleaning small cartons, staple each shut. Draw a chimney on a folded piece of red construction paper. Cut out and add details to the two chimney cutouts with black marker. Staple the chimney cutouts, one on each side, to the top of the milk carton. Glue thick, straight pretzels in place, breaking "logs" to fit around the door and chimney. Avoid nibbling by planning a "termite party" to clean up the leftovers.

A Unique Bird

Students will enjoy making their own unique penguins. Each student will need:

construction paper:

- 2" x 12" piece of black
- 1 1/2" x 6" piece of black
- 1 1/2" x 6" piece of white
- 1" x 5" piece of black
- 1" x 5" piece of white
- 2" x 3" piece of black
- 3" x 3" square of orange

other supplies:

scissors, glue, hole punch, black crayon

Directions:

1. Roll the 2" x 12" and the 1" x 5" pieces of black into cylinders and glue. Glue the two cylinders together to make the head and body. Crease the lower portion of the body as shown.
2. Round the corners at one end of the 1 1/2" x 6" piece of white; then glue to the front of the body.
3. Fold in half the 1 1/2" x 6" piece of black. Cut out two matching wings.
4. Fold in half the 1" x 5" piece of white. Cut out two matching wings. Glue each cutout atop a black wing.
5. Glue the wings to the body.
6. Fold in half the orange square. Cut out two matching feet. Glue feet to the body.
7. Trim the 2" x 3" piece of black to make a tail. Glue to the body. Crease the tail as shown.
8. Using a hole punch and a scrap of white, make two eyes. Add details with crayon. Glue eyes to head.
9. Cut a beak from a scrap of orange. Glue to head.

Steps 1 & 2

fold

wings
Steps 3 & 4

Step 7
back

glue →

fold up

©1990 The Education Center, Inc.

71

Abe Mobiles

Honor the birthday of Abraham Lincoln by making an eye-catching mobile of the president himself! Have each student fold a 12" x 18" piece of black construction paper in half lengthwise and cut as shown. Students design face parts from the paper scraps and hang using thread.

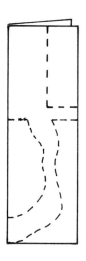

Famous Person Paper Weaving

History will be alive in your room with this colorful weaving display. Cut a supply of 12" x 1/2" red and white construction paper strips. Give each child a 12" x 18" sheet of blue construction paper. The child folds the paper in half and cuts at 3/4" intervals from the fold to within two inches of the edge. Then the child weaves red and white strips alternately through the unfolded blue paper, glues the strips down at the edges, and lets the weaving dry. Have each student choose a Lincoln, Washington, or Martin Luther King, Jr., silhouette (pages 73–75) to trace in the center of a 12" x 18" sheet of black construction paper. After cutting out the silhouette, the student glues the resulting outline onto his woven mat.

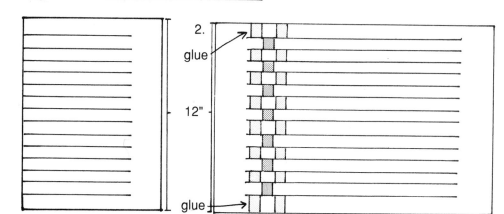

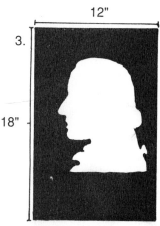

©1990 The Education Center, Inc.

©1990 The Education Center, Inc.

Pattern

Use with "Famous Person Paper Weaving" on page

©1990 The Education Center, Inc.

Pattern
Use with "Famous Per[

do we need Pinocchio ?
P. 3⁶ 3⁷

ohl gov Keating

©1990 The Education Center, Inc.

Conversation Hearts

Share some conversation hearts with your youngsters and send them off to the art area to make a few chatty hearts of their own. Cut sponges into heart shapes and clip a clothespin to one side of each. Pour a little white tempera paint into several pie pans. Tint the white paint in each pan to a pastel shade by blending in a tiny bit of red, yellow, blue, green, purple, or orange paint. Have students dunk the sponges into the paints and print heart designs on art paper. Encourage students to try overlapping the prints slightly for interesting effects. After the prints have dried, have students use felt-tip markers to add a Valentine's Day message to each heart print.

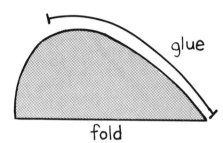

glue

fold

Valentine Mouse

Trap students' interest with these valentine mice treats. For each mouse, cut a five-inch, red square of construction paper or felt into a heart. Glue the top edge as shown. Cut and glue on two heart ears. Add wiggly eyes; then color a nose and whiskers. Insert a valentine pencil from The Education Center or a lollipop so that the end sticks out for a tail. Add a message on the mouse if desired. *or use yarn for a tail*

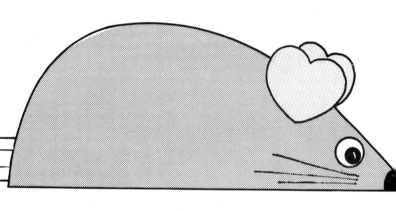

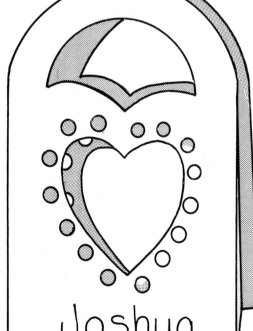

Joshua

Valentine Bags

Treat your students to special Valentine sacks. With the sack flat, fold it vertically along the center. Cut a handle at the top. Add to the cut design by using a paper punch. Decorate with markers, cut paper, stickers, or crayons. Personalize each sack with the student's name.

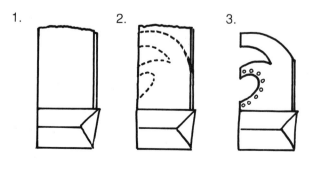

1.   2.   3.

©1990 The Education Center, Inc.

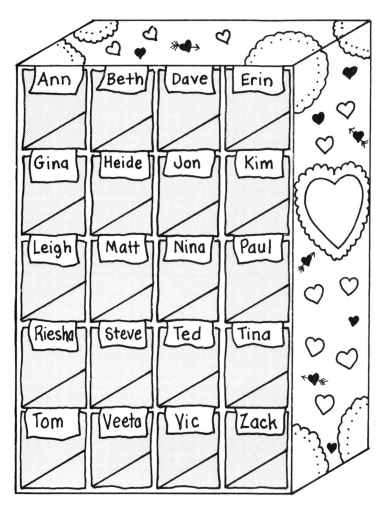

Class Valentine Mailbox

Boxes from a local liquor store can furnish you with a perfect class valentine mailbox. Glue several boxes with dividers together (enough so that each student will have his own "mailbox"). Have students decorate the class mailbox with red paper, foil, doilies, tissue paper, and other materials. Tape a name tag to the top of each small mailbox. Not only does this facilitate the job of distributing valentines, but later you can also use the box to reinforce alphabetical order or other sequencing skills.

Valentine Mailboxes For The School

Thinking of sending a valentine to a special someone at your school, but alas, they have no mailbox? Your students can solve this dilemma and ensure that the entire school staff is remembered on Valentine's Day. As a class project, have groups of students construct mailboxes for the librarian, school counselor, school nurse, teaching specialists, bus drivers, and cafeteria, office, and custodial workers.

Ask children to make an alphabetical listing of all of the school personnel. Duplicate the list for other classes. Before Valentine's Day, your class can make heart-shaped name tags for these special people. This will help children to identify those familiar faces by name when they write their valentines. The whole school will take notice!

Then have student groups cover grocery boxes with aluminum foil. Students decorate the boxes by gluing overlapping, tissue paper hearts to the foil and adding the appropriate staff name or names. Place the mailboxes in the school lobby or other convenient location so that students from all classes can add their valentines.

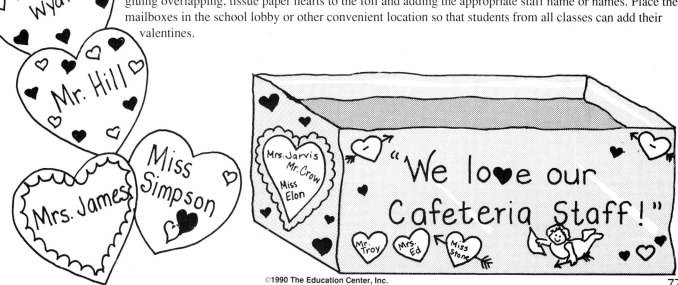

©1990 The Education Center, Inc.

77

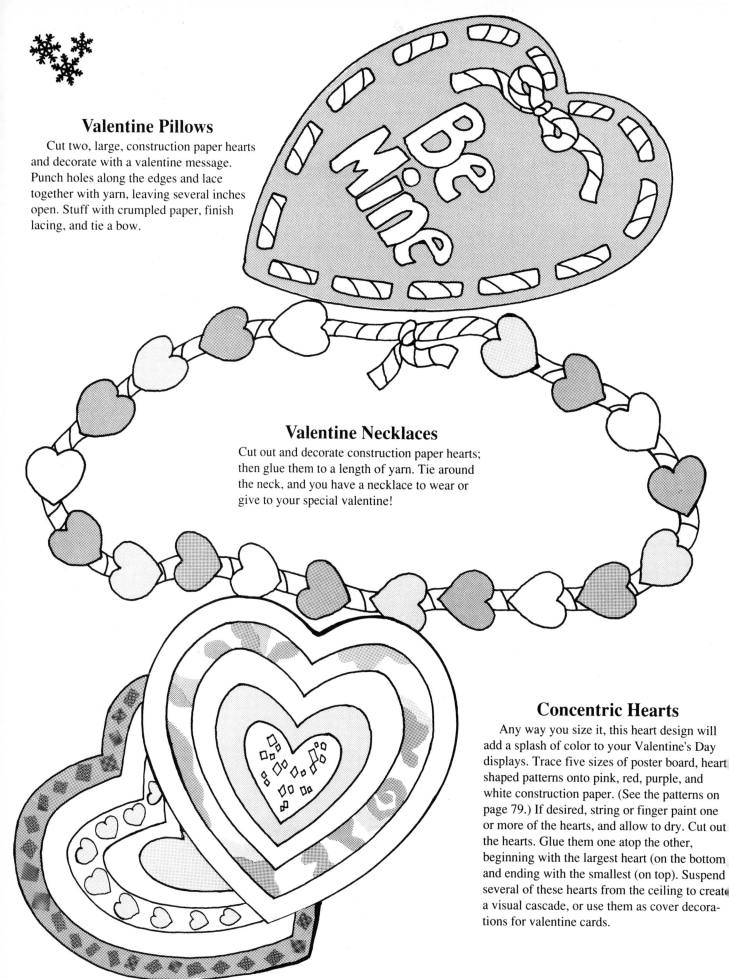

Valentine Pillows

Cut two, large, construction paper hearts and decorate with a valentine message. Punch holes along the edges and lace together with yarn, leaving several inches open. Stuff with crumpled paper, finish lacing, and tie a bow.

Valentine Necklaces

Cut out and decorate construction paper hearts; then glue them to a length of yarn. Tie around the neck, and you have a necklace to wear or give to your special valentine!

Concentric Hearts

Any way you size it, this heart design will add a splash of color to your Valentine's Day displays. Trace five sizes of poster board, heart shaped patterns onto pink, red, purple, and white construction paper. (See the patterns on page 79.) If desired, string or finger paint one or more of the hearts, and allow to dry. Cut out the hearts. Glue them one atop the other, beginning with the largest heart (on the bottom) and ending with the smallest (on top). Suspend several of these hearts from the ceiling to create a visual cascade, or use them as cover decorations for valentine cards.

©1990 The Education Center, Inc.

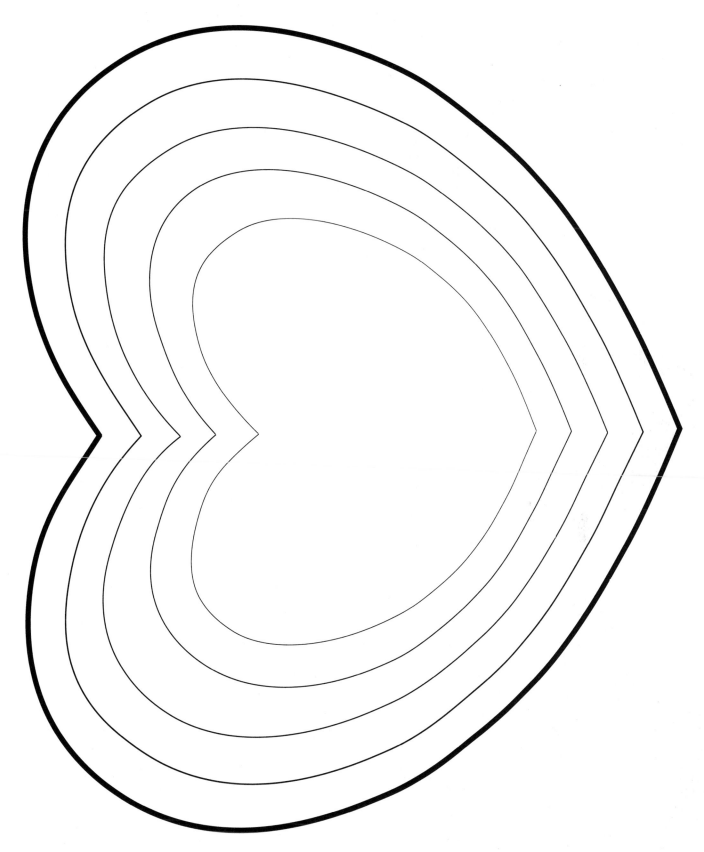

©1990 The Education Center, Inc.

Quilled Hearts

You can use a pencil and paper strips to turn a plain heart into a fancy masterpiece. Cut 12" x 1/2" strips of construction paper. Let each student cut out a large heart. (See the patterns on page 79.) To fill in the heart, the student wraps a strip around his pencil, slides it off, and glues it—standing on edge—to the heart. Tell children to hold each quilled strip in place until the glue has dried enough to hold. Little hands will find one-inch-wide strips easier to handle. Use the same idea with other seasonal shapes—pumpkins, lambs, apples, flowers, eggs, turkeys.

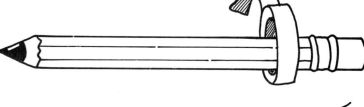

Valentine Bookmarks

One snip of the scissors and you have a gift for Valentine's Day—a valentine bookmark. Cut a heart-shaped corner from an envelope. Decorate, and you've got a nifty bookmark that slips right over the corner of a page. A great gift idea for other seasons, too!

A Different Valentine

Make a colorful checkerboard pattern with crayon or marker on a 4 1/2" x 6" piece of graph paper. Then fold a 6" x 9" piece of construction paper in half. Cut a heart from the top half. Paste the graph design inside to show through the heart opening. Add a message, and you've got a really different valentine!

©1990 The Education Center, Inc.

Valentine Baskets

These paper baskets are filled with mixed-up, valentine messages. Provide many colors of construction paper, white paper strips, and a heart pattern (see page 79). Each child traces the pattern on a folded piece of red construction paper and cuts out the two resulting hearts. The student glues the hearts together the lower edges, leaving the top open. He then glues a paper handle inside one heart and decorates his basket with paper scraps. Finally, have the child write each word of his valentine message on a white strip, then decorate one end of each strip with additional hearts. The child completes his basket by inserting the strips in his basket, ready to give to his special valentine!

"Thumbody" Loves You!

Have each student cut a heart from folded paper, placing one edge on the fold so the heart will open. Children decorate the fronts of their cards using red ink thumbprints and permanent markers. Encourage students to add valentine messages on the fronts of and inside their cards.

©1990 The Education Center, Inc.

Hanging Hearts

This heart can be worn by a special valentine. Each student needs fifteen 3" x 3" squares of red or pink construction paper. The student stacks his squares into groups of three and glues them together. Next he cuts a heart shape from one glued set. This heart is then used as a pattern for the four remaining sets. Punch a matching hole near the top of each set. The holes and edges of the five hearts are matched and glued together. The student may write a valentine message on the top heart if he wishes. After the heart has dried completely, the student sands the edges smooth with sandpaper and coats the back surface with a generous amount of white glue. When the heart is completely dry, he coats the front and edges. A second coat of glue will provide added strength and protection. Insert a length of yarn or chain to wear.

Valentine Magazine Mosaics

For a unique mosaic project with a lot of heart, provide students with four or five heart patterns in different sizes. (See the patterns on page 79.) On a sheet of white paper, the student traces each pattern once, overlapping the hearts occasionally to create an interesting design. To complete the project, have the student tear pieces of colored paper from old magazines, selecting related values and colors. The child glues similarly colored pieces in each enclosed area of the design. Mount finished mosaics on construction paper and display with pride!

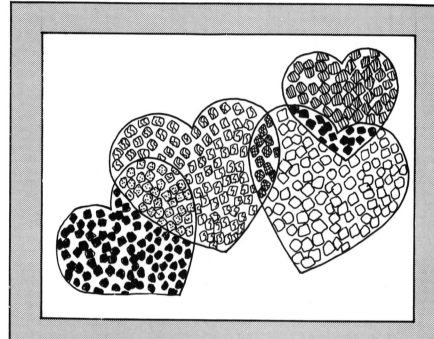

Valentine Flowers

Brighten your room with a colorful display of valentine flower arrangements. Each child cuts out several red and pink construction paper hearts, green construction paper leaves and stems, and a blue construction paper vase. Students arrange their pieces on 9" x 12" sheets of white construction paper and glue in place.

82

©1990 The Education Center, Inc.

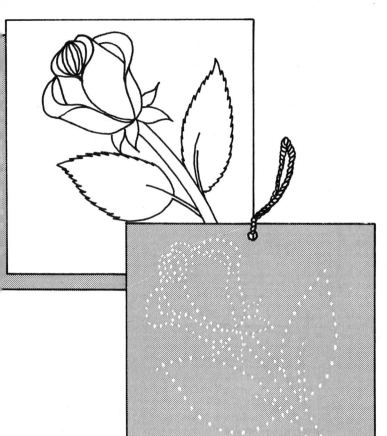

Pin Art

Decorate for Valentine's Day with a different kind of window hanging. Clip a simple picture to red construction paper. With a straight pin, punch holes 1/4" apart through both papers along the outline. Remove the picture when completed, and hang or tape the pin-punched outline in the window.

Valentine Pockets

Before Valentine's Day comes, show students how to make their own valentine pockets from 12" x 18" sheets of red and white construction paper.

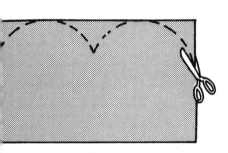

1. Cut one long side of the red paper to form the top of a heart.

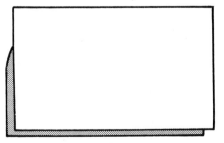

2. Place the white sheet on top of the red.

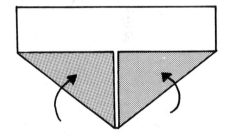

3. Fold both bottom corners up to the center to form the point of the heart.

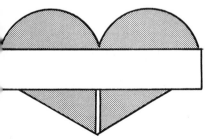

4. Fold the remaining white paper down to reveal the top of the heart.

5. Fold the excess white paper back and staple.

6. Label the white flap with your name, and decorate if desired.

©1990 The Education Center, Inc.

How Big Is Your Heart?

No doubt you've heard of a heart as big as all outdoors. But have you ever seen one? To begin making this giant heart, cut a heart shape from bulletin board paper. Draw a grid to divide the heart shape into squares (at least one square per student). On a pink or white paper square the same size as those on the heart cutout, have each student draw a picture using several heart designs. Glue the squares to the grid, trimming off the excess paper around the perimeter of the heart shape. Mount the cutout on a bulletin board. Staple red rickrack to cover the seams between the squares. Gather white crepe paper streamers, tucking them behind the heart shape, and stapling them into place as a frilly ruffle.

Valentine Triple Weave

As your class experiments with different types of weaving, they'll be creating a great-looking bulletin board display, too! Each student needs three squares of construction paper. Students fold pieces in half and cut a different type of weaving line in each (straight, wavy, and diagonal). Using construction paper strips, students weave their squares. To complete his project, each student cuts a large heart from one woven pattern, and progressively smaller hearts from each of the two remaining patterns. Hearts are glued around edges and on top of one another as shown. For contrast, students may wish to cut different shapes from their smallest weaving cutouts.

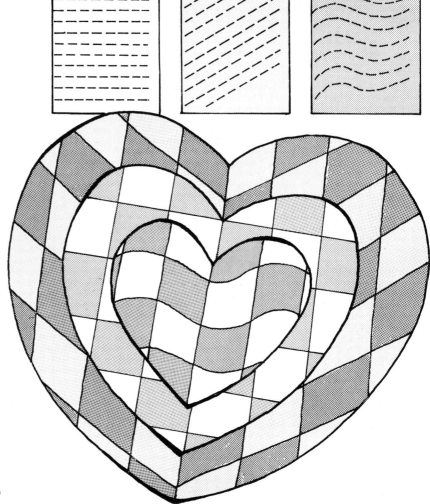

84

©1990 The Education Center, Inc.

To
My
Special
Valentine!
Be Mine!

Valentine Pop-up Card

To make a special Valentine's Day card, fold a cut-out heart as shown and glue to the inside center of a construction paper card. Decorate, add a holiday poem or message, and send your original, pop-up card special delivery!

1.

2. fold

3. fold

4. open

5. Invert the V-fold.

6. Glue to center of card.

Party Cups

Make a party favor for every month of the year! Duplicate the pattern on page 86 on construction paper. Let students write their names on the hearts and decorate them with crayons or markers. Cut out on the solid lines of the grid and fold on the dotted lines. Staple the sides to make a cup to fill with candy or nuts. Use the same pattern each month by changing the top decoration to suit the holiday or season.

©1990 The Education Center, Inc.

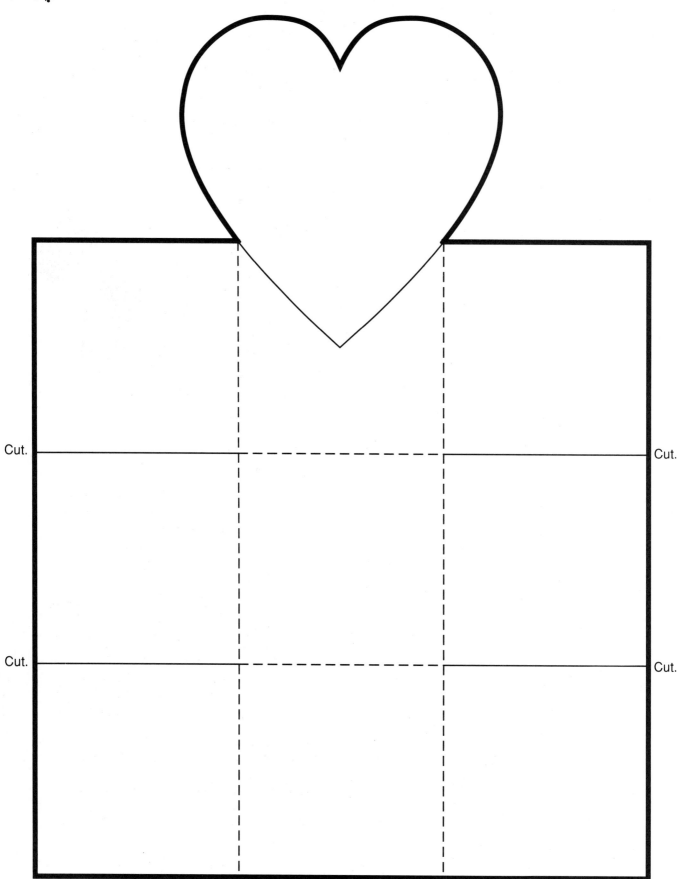

Cut.

Cut.

Cut.

Cut.

©1990 The Education Center, Inc.

Spring

Spring Lambs

Welcome spring with a flock of woolly lambs! Have each student trace his hand on black construction paper and cut out the shape. The child glues a wiggly eye on the thumb and cotton balls to fill in the body. Each black sheep gets a colorful bow on its neck.

Flowering Raindrops

Capture the beauty of spring flowers in colorful raindrops. Cut two large identical raindrops from wax paper. Arrange tissue paper blooms and leaves on one of the raindrops, attaching with tiny bits of paste until the design is complete. Place the second raindrop over the first, sandwiching the flowers between the raindrops. Press with an iron set at a low temperature. Hang the completed raindrops in windows or from the ceiling.

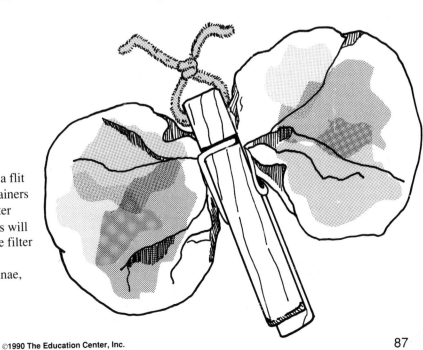

Clothespin Butterflies

These eye-catching butterflies can be created in just a flit and a flutter! Use food coloring to prepare several containers of differently colored water. Using an eyedropper, scatter drops of colored water onto a round coffee filter. Colors will absorb and blend, creating an interesting design. Let the filter dry. Beginning in the center, carefully gather the filter together as shown and clip with a clothespin. For antennae, twist and attach a length of pipe cleaner.

©1990 The Education Center, Inc.

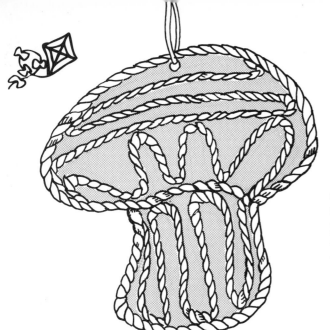

Swinging Designs

Draw a simple pencil design on newsprint, incorporating some swirling inside the shape. Lay a sheet of wax paper on top of the design. Saturate two-foot lengths of jute twine in wallpaper paste and place over the pencil lines. When dry, peel the jute off the wax paper and glue colored tissue paper behind the design. Add a string and hang from the ceiling—real swinging artwork!

Flower Frame

Frame student photos inside gigantic blooms and send them home as greeting cards. Duplicate the flower card pattern (page 89) onto white construction paper, and cut on the dotted line with an X-acto knife. Have each student color and cut out the flower and leaf patterns. Instruct students to attach construction paper leaves as shown, after folding the flowers on the solid lines. Have students trace or write greetings inside their cards. Or have them glue in copies of the poem (page 89). Glue a photocopy of each child's school photo to the center of his flower as shown.

Color Burst Bouquets

These crayon bouquets simply "burst" with color! Using a zigzag motion, color small, medium, and large circles of differing colors on art paper to create each flower. Color heavily to create deep colors; then cut out the bouquet. Cut out a flowerpot shape from construction paper. Fold the cutout in half; then cut out shapes on the fold to make a design. Attach a piece of wallpaper, construction paper, or tissue paper to the back of the flowerpot, then glue the bouquet to the flowerpot. Now isn't that a pretty sight?

©1990 The Education Center, Inc.

Patterns

Use with "Flower Frame" on page 88.

I am like a flower
That's raised with love by you.
You help me grow up big and strong.
Mom, thanks for all you do.

Finished Frame

©1990 The Education Center, Inc.

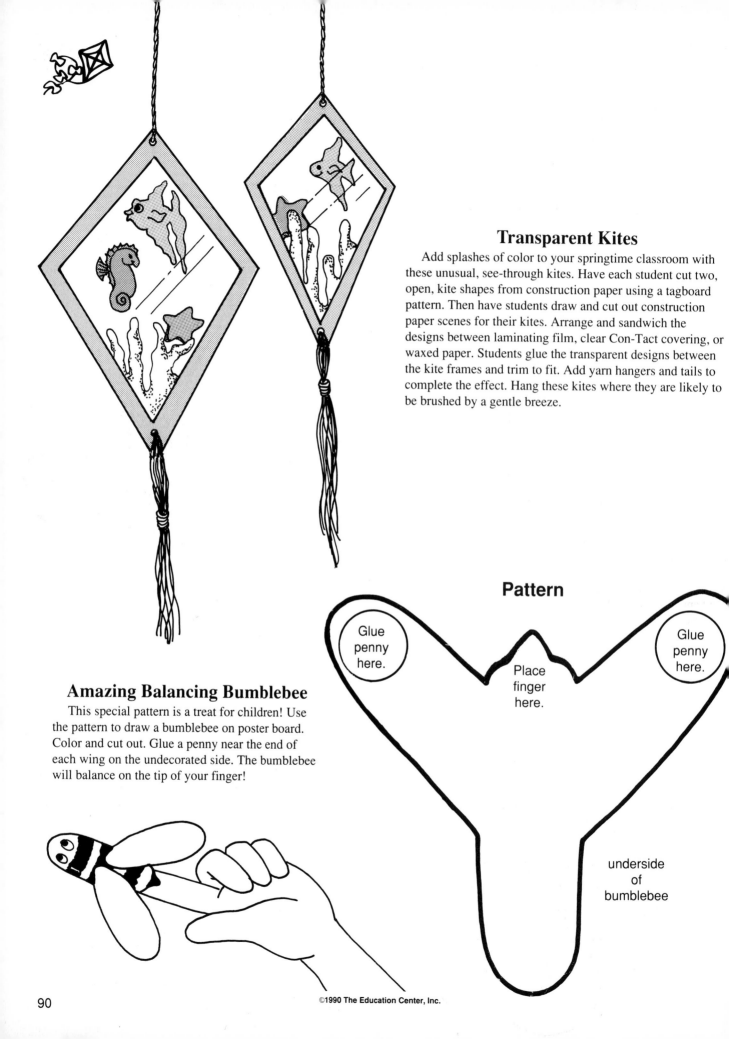

Transparent Kites

Add splashes of color to your springtime classroom with these unusual, see-through kites. Have each student cut two, open, kite shapes from construction paper using a tagboard pattern. Then have students draw and cut out construction paper scenes for their kites. Arrange and sandwich the designs between laminating film, clear Con-Tact covering, or waxed paper. Students glue the transparent designs between the kite frames and trim to fit. Add yarn hangers and tails to complete the effect. Hang these kites where they are likely to be brushed by a gentle breeze.

Pattern

Glue penny here.

Place finger here.

Glue penny here.

Amazing Balancing Bumblebee

This special pattern is a treat for children! Use the pattern to draw a bumblebee on poster board. Color and cut out. Glue a penny near the end of each wing on the undecorated side. The bumblebee will balance on the tip of your finger!

underside of bumblebee

90

©1990 The Education Center, Inc.

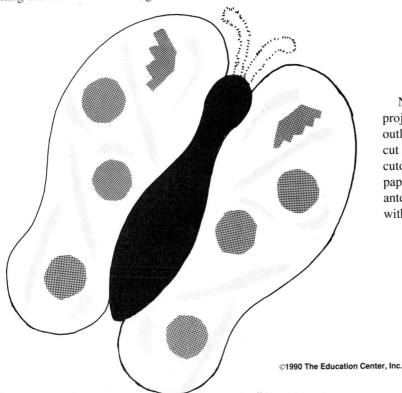

Popcorn Flowers

To make realistic snapdragons and bluebonnets, pop some popcorn. Make different-colored "blooms" by putting the popped corn in a bag with powdered tempera and shaking. Draw stems or glue paper stems on your paper; then add the colored popcorn. (Be sure to caution students not to eat the colored popcorn!) While you're at it, make some fresh popcorn for students to enjoy after finishing their project.

Caterpillar Capers

This little caterpillar is going to munch his way into our classroom. Enlarge a leaf pattern on page 14; then trace the outline onto green construction paper and cut out. Shake five cotton balls in a Ziploc bag containing brown powdered tempera paint. Glue the cotton balls on the leaf cutout and attach construction paper antennae and eyes. Complete the effect by cutting a "bite" out of the leaf with pinking shears. Ummm-mmm, good!

Butterfly, Bat Your Wings!

No doubt, your students will jump into this butterfly project with both feet. To make a butterfly, trace the outlines of both of your shoes onto construction paper and cut them out. Decorate with markers. Transform the foot cutouts into wings by gluing them to a black construction paper butterfly body as shown. Glue on pipe cleaner antennae. Double the fun by displaying these butterflies with the caterpillars from "Caterpillar Capers" on this page.

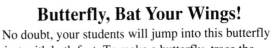

©1990 The Education Center, Inc.

91

Paper Plate Craft

Encourage your students to dish up their creativity as they cut paper plates for a springtime art project. Provide paper plates, scissors, glue, crayons or markers, and colored paper for features. Show some sample creatures, and let them snip, glue, and decorate their own.

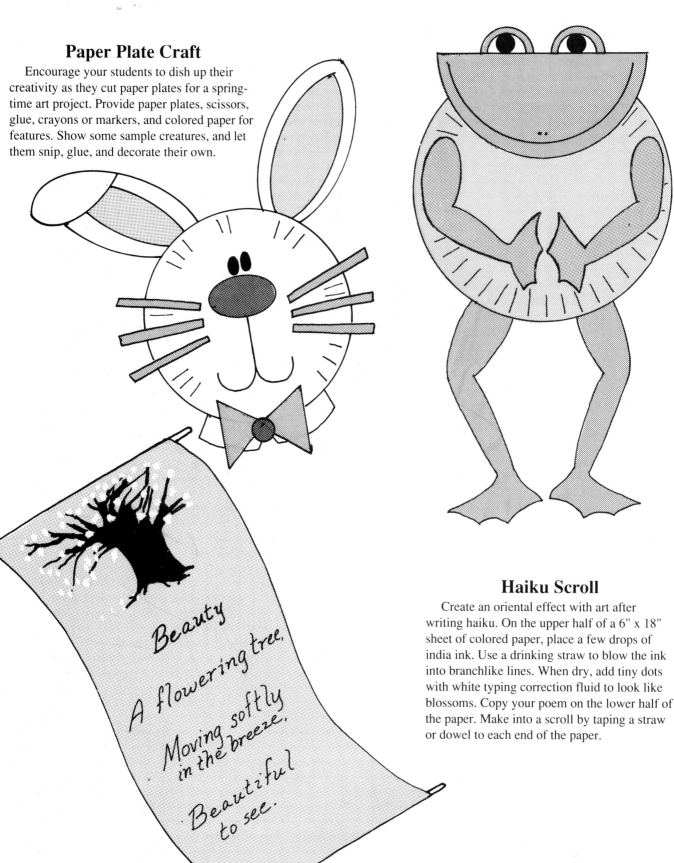

Beauty
A flowering tree,
Moving softly
in the breeze,
Beautiful
to see.

Haiku Scroll

Create an oriental effect with art after writing haiku. On the upper half of a 6" x 18" sheet of colored paper, place a few drops of india ink. Use a drinking straw to blow the ink into branchlike lines. When dry, add tiny dots with white typing correction fluid to look like blossoms. Copy your poem on the lower half of the paper. Make into a scroll by taping a straw or dowel to each end of the paper.

©1990 The Education Center, Inc.

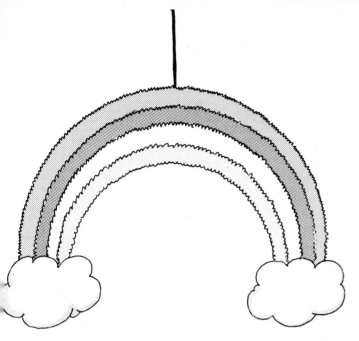

Rainbows For Springtime

Colorful hanging rainbows welcome springtime to your classroom. Provide each student with four brightly colored pipe cleaners with chenille stems, glue, cotton, and plastic fishing line. Have the student form each pipe cleaner into a circle shape, allowing it to spring back to form an arc. Glue the four curved pipe cleaners together to form a rainbow. Add a puffy cotton cloud at each end. Suspend from the lights or ceiling with fishing line.

Three-D Flowers

Spread spring fever with this colorful craft. Cut a Styrofoam cup in half lengthwise and glue to a piece of cardboard. Glue colorful buttons for flower centers. Cut out small petals and leaves, crease down the center, and glue in place. Add stems with a green marker.

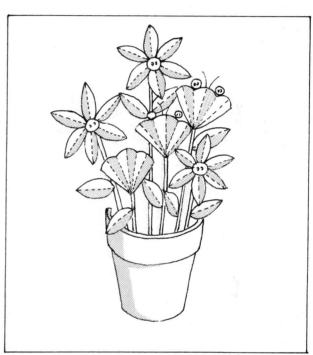

Feathered Finger Puppets

Young chidren can make finger puppets to use with the rhyme below. Roll and tape white construction paper around little fingers. Paste on a paper beak and eyes and feather-duster plumage as shown.

Five little chickadees sitting on a limb,
One flew away when a jay frightened him.
Four little chickadees sitting on a limb,
One flew away to watch a wood duck swim.
Three little chickadees sitting on a limb,
One flew away when a beetle tickled him.
Two little chickadees sitting on a limb,
One flew away when a cat threatened him.
One little chickadee alone on the limb,
Flew home to safety as daylight dimmed.

©1990 The Education Center, Inc.

Styrofoam Egg Carton Flowers

Save various colors of Styrofoam egg cartons for this colorful, cut-and-paste spring garden.

Materials needed for each student:
9" x 12" construction paper
construction paper scraps
two egg carton cups per flower
glue
scissors

Directions:
1. To make one flower, cut an egg carton cup from the edge to within 3/4 inch of the center of the cup.
2. Make 4–8 more cuts in the same manner.
3. Place the flattened cut piece on the construction paper, and glue it down.
4. Cut a second cup, with less petals than the first. Glue it to the center of the first cup without flattening it.
5. Cut and add paper stems and leaves to finish the picture.

Hanging Butterflies

Hang these three-dimensional butterflies to flutter in the breeze. Duplicate the pattern on page 95. Color the entire butterfly; then glue it on colored construction paper. Cut out the butterfly and fold on the solid lines. Cut on the dotted lines. Alternate pulling and pushing the strips to make 3-D butterfly wings. Add paper antennae.

©1990 The Education Center, Inc.

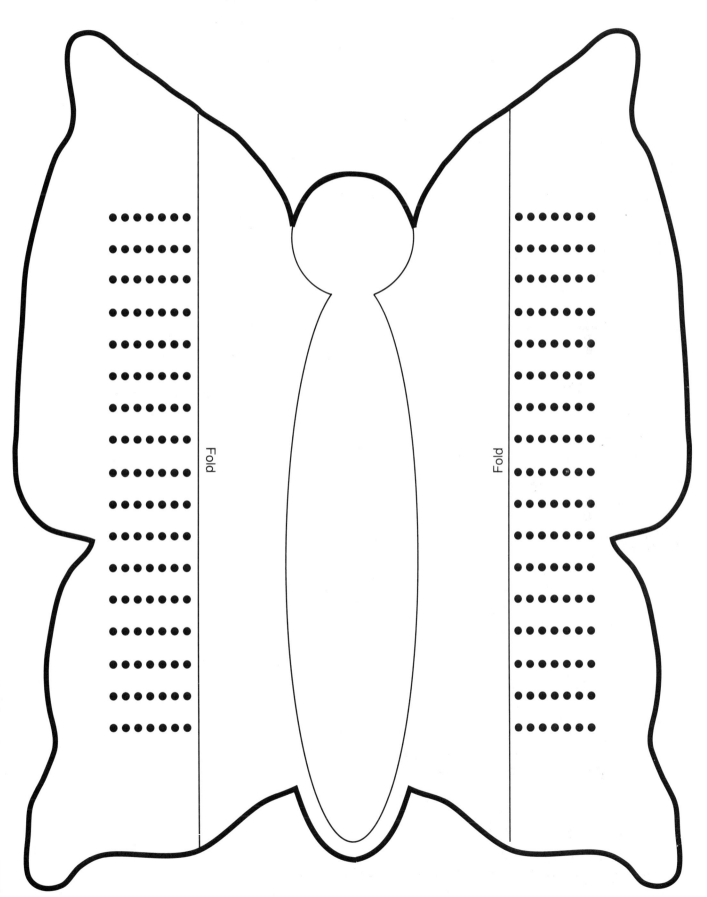

Fold

Fold

©1990 The Education Center, Inc.

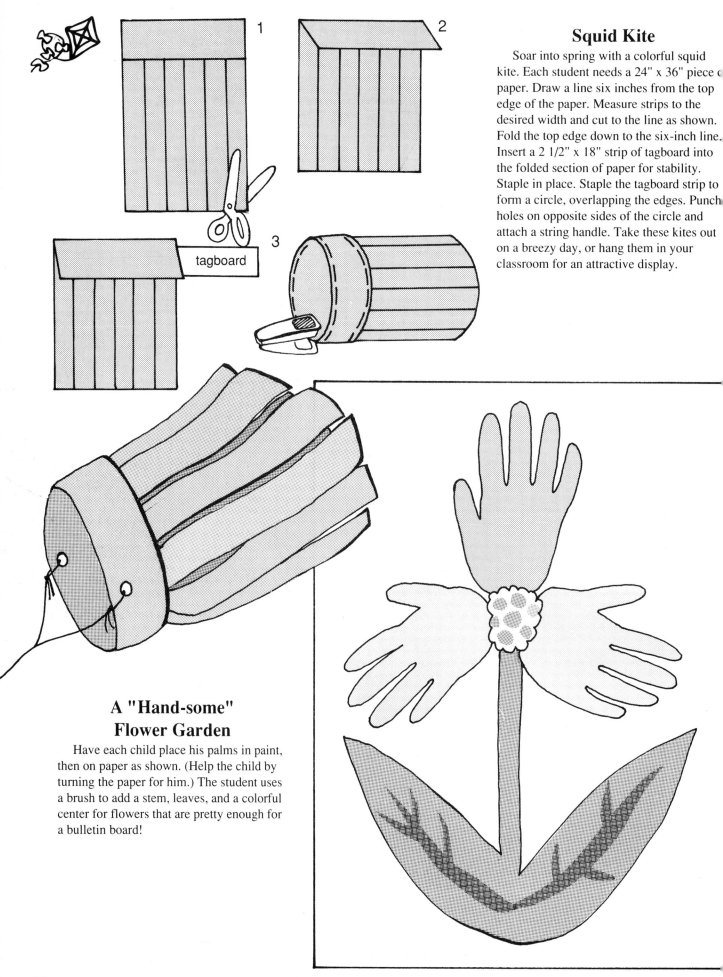

Squid Kite

Soar into spring with a colorful squid kite. Each student needs a 24" x 36" piece of paper. Draw a line six inches from the top edge of the paper. Measure strips to the desired width and cut to the line as shown. Fold the top edge down to the six-inch line. Insert a 2 1/2" x 18" strip of tagboard into the folded section of paper for stability. Staple in place. Staple the tagboard strip to form a circle, overlapping the edges. Punch holes on opposite sides of the circle and attach a string handle. Take these kites out on a breezy day, or hang them in your classroom for an attractive display.

tagboard

A "Hand-some" Flower Garden

Have each child place his palms in paint, then on paper as shown. (Help the child by turning the paper for him.) The student uses a brush to add a stem, leaves, and a colorful center for flowers that are pretty enough for a bulletin board!

©1990 The Education Center, Inc.

Pussy Willows

For a spring art project, make a vase of pussy willows, using wallpaper and puffed wheat. Glue a vase cut from a wallpaper scrap onto a piece of construction paper. Use dark markers or crayons to draw the stems; then glue on puffed wheat to look like pussy willows. If possible, display a real pussy willow branch to help children place the puffed wheat correctly.

Clothespin Lambs

Your students can make their own little lambs from clothespins, tongue depressors, wiggle eyes, and fluffy fleece or cotton. Begin by having each student clip two spring-type clothespins to a tongue depressor. Then have students paint the tongue depressor and the clothespins black. Instruct each student to staple or glue fleece or cotton around the tongue depressor. Have students glue a wiggle eye to each side of the "head" as shown.

Cellophane Sun Catchers

Create dazzling springtime sun catchers. On construction paper, duplicate one white and one green copy of the pattern (page 98). On the white copy, color the flowerpot, flowers, leaves, stems, and frame. Cut inside the frame and around the pot and plants on both copies. Sparingly put glue on the back of the colored copy; then place it on a colorful sheet of cellophane. Glue the green copy to the back of the cellophane in the same manner. For added stability, staple each corner. Trim the excess cellophane. Suspend the sun catchers from the ceiling, or attach them to your windows to add radiant colors to your classroom.

©1990 The Education Center, Inc.

©1990 The Education Center, Inc.

Dried Creations

Plan ahead and make beautiful bookmarks or stationery from dried flowers, leaves, and weeds. In early spring, ask students to bring in items to dry. Place items between the pages of a large catalog.

Materials needed: white paper, waxed paper, facial tissues (any color), glue, water, scissors, large paintbrushes, and dried materials

Cut a supply of white paper: 2" x 8" for bookmarks and 8 1/2" x 5 1/2" for stationery or cards. Glue the corners of the white paper to a piece of waxed paper. Trim the waxed paper to the same size as the white paper. On a desk, arrange the dried materials into a desired pattern. Brush the waxed paper with a mixture of two parts glue to one part water; then carefully lay the dried materials on the glued surface. Place a single tissue (separate a two-ply tissue) on top of the project. Carefully dab the glue mixture on top of the tissue covering the project. The tissue will wrinkle. Continue to apply the glue mixture slightly beyond the waxed paper edges, making sure the tissue is entirely moistened. Allow the project to dry until crisp. Trim off the excess tissue, and your project is complete.

April Showers Mobile

Children can make umbrella mobiles to welcome those ny days! Trace the umbrella, handle, and raindrop terns on page 100 on poster board. (You will need to ce approximately nine raindrops.) Cut out the pieces. corate the umbrella if desired. To form the umbrella, l edge A over edge B, and tape or glue together. Punch a le in the top of the handle at the X. Tie a length of yarn ough the hole; then slip the other end of the yarn through umbrella top. Tie on a paper clip for hanging. Fasten ch raindrop to the umbrella with thread.

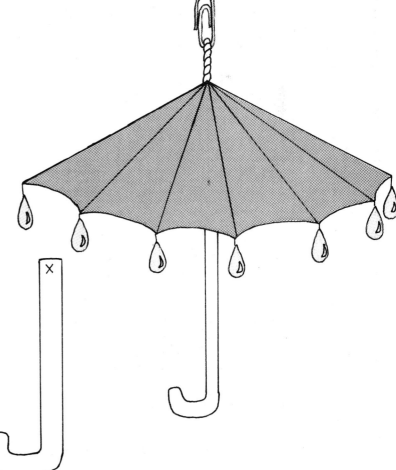

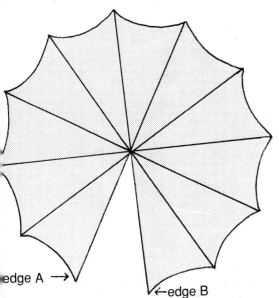

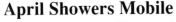

edge A →

←edge B

©1990 The Education Center, Inc.

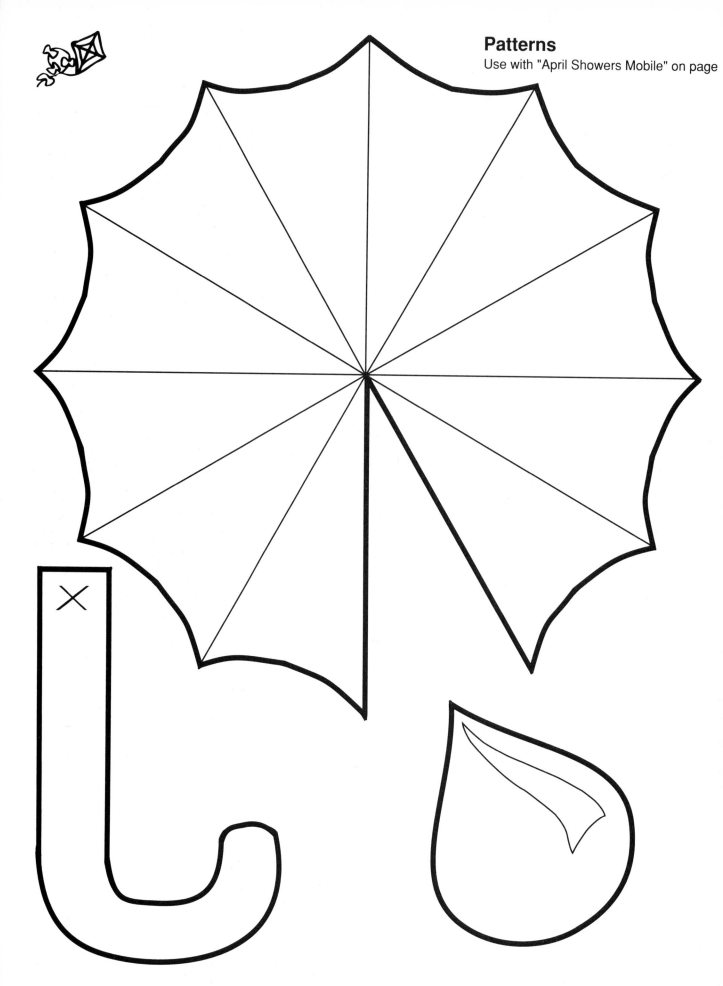

©1990 The Education Center, Inc.

Rainbow Mobiles

Bring a bit of spring into your room with colorful, rainbow mobiles. For each rainbow, cut a small paper plate in half. Cut an arch in the bottom of the plate to make a rainbow. Roll small squares of tissue paper into balls and glue to the plates in arches. Glue cotton to the end of each rainbow to make a cloud. Punch a hole in the top of the rainbow, add yarn, and hang from the classroom ceiling.

Three-D Butterflies

Make 3-D butterflies for your windows or ceiling h this tissue paper project. Glue torn pieces of orful tissue on the end sections of a plastic six-pack k holder. These will form the wings. Glue torn ces of black tissue to the center sections for the ly. After gluing, fold the rings as shown and le. Complete by adding paper antennae.

Barnyard Chicks

Invite a barnyard full of chicks to your classroom and you won't hear a peep! Have each student cut a large egg shape from yellow construction paper. Also on yellow construction paper, have students trace and cut out the outlines of their hands. Have students use brads to fasten the hand cutouts to the egg cutouts as shown. From orange construction paper, have students cut out legs and feet and a diamond shape. Have students glue the legs to the back of the egg cutout. Then have children fold the diamond-shaped cutout in half and glue it to the egg cutout as a beak. Students complete their chicks by drawing eyes or gluing on wiggle eyes.

©1990 The Education Center, Inc.

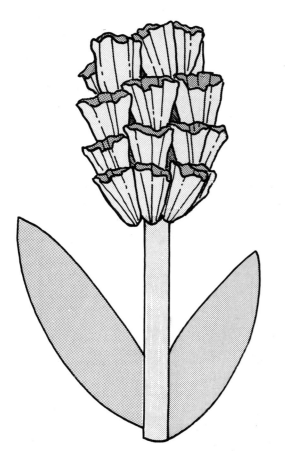

Fresh Spring Hyacinths

Your classroom will bloom with these spring flowers. Each child needs a toi paper tube, scissors, glue, 1 1/2-inch squares of purple and pink tissue paper, a pencil, floral tape, a plastic straw, and construction paper. Staple one end of the tube and cut it to a rounded shape. Cover the tube with the tissue by folding each square, one at a time, over the end of a pencil. Dab each piece lightly in glue an attach to the tube. Wind floral tape around a plastic straw and attach as a stem. Add construction paper leaves. "Plant" these pretty flowers in paper cups or pos on a bulletin board.

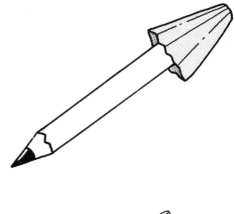

St. Patrick's Day Mobiles

Fill your room with personalized St. Patrick's Day mobiles. Have each student write a letter of his name on a small white shamrock (pattern on page 105) and glue it onto a larger green shamrock. The student should make enough of these shamrocks to spell his name. After punching a hole in the top and bottom of each finished shamrock, the child strings them together with green yarn. Hang these in your room to add a touch of St. Patrick's Day spirit!

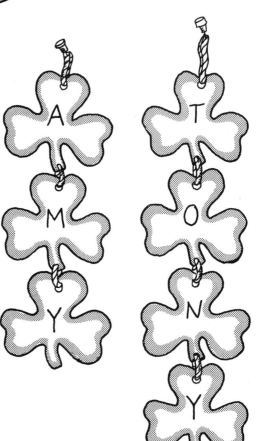

©1990 The Education Center, Inc.

Peanut Pals

Make a peanut pal for St. Patrick's Day! Pick the end out of a shell and shake the peanuts out. Dye the shell in green food coloring. Complete the little finger puppet with markers and felt bits.

Stained Glass Shamrocks

Hang stained glass shamrocks in your windows for glowing St. Patrick's Day decorations. Use a foil-covered warming tray to melt several crayons. Swirl the mixture slightly; then place a sheet of paper on top and rub across the back of the paper. Remove, let cool, and cut out shamrock shapes using the pattern on page 105.

Shamrock Necklaces

Get the entire class into the St. Patrick's Day mood with these shamrock necklaces. Provide a shamrock pattern (page 105) and have students trace it on cardboard. Cut out the shamrock shapes or have the students cut them out. Have students smooth glue onto their cutouts to secure pieces of dry spaghetti. When dry, trim off excess spaghetti around the edges. Students paint their shamrocks green and later brush on a thin layer of glue as a glaze. Use a needle to string with green yarn.

©1990 The Education Center, Inc.

103

Woven Greenery

Weave a special shamrock for a St. Patrick's decoration. Use shamrock cutouts (pattern on page 105) and narrow strips of contrasting paper. Students fold shamrocks in half and cut slits from the fold to about 1/2" from the edges. Then they open the shamrocks and weave color strips in and out of the slits. For a finishing touch, have students add a holiday greeting or staple a tiny shamrock to the bottom of each woven strip.

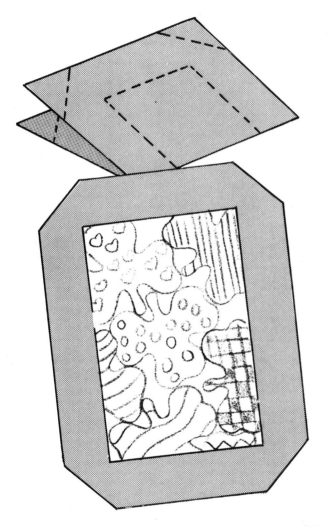

Classy Clover

Here is a quiet art activity that children love! Provide each stude with a tagboard clover pattern (page 105), two sheets of 9" x 12" construction paper (one green, one white), a green marker, glue, an scissors. Instruct the student to fill the white paper with clover desig by randomly tracing the pattern with the green marker. Next have t student decorate each clover with a different design. To make a fra have the child fold the green construction paper in half and cut as shown. The student then glues the clover design behind the green fr and trims the edges.

Shamrock Hounds

Decorate your room for St. Patrick's Day with student-made shamrock hounds. Using the patterns and directions on page 105, duplicate all the pieces on construction paper. Students cut out pieces and assemble their shamrock hounds. They add details with crayons.

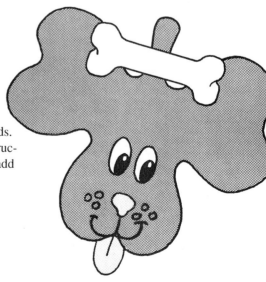

   ©1990 The Education Center, Inc.

Patterns

Use with "Stained Glass Shamrocks" on page 103, "Woven Greenery" on page 104, and "Classy Clover" on page 104.

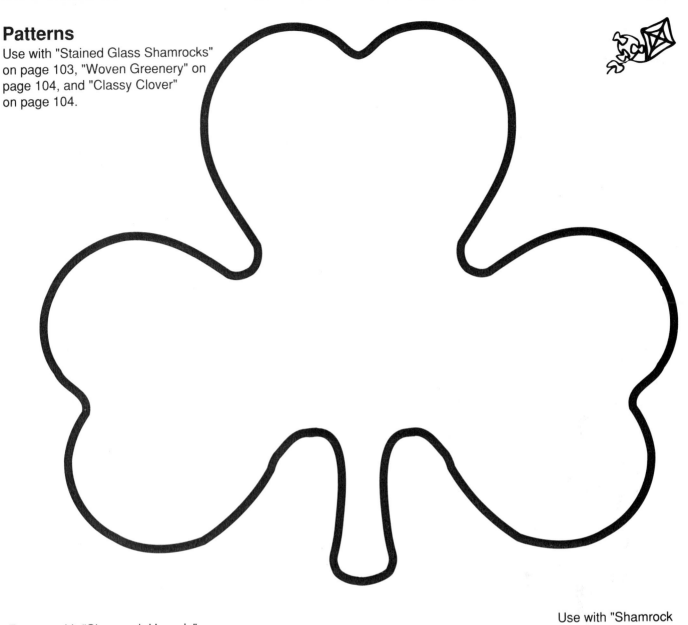

For use with "Shamrock Hounds" on page 104, duplicate the large shamrock on green, the tongue on red, the nose on brown, the eyes on white, and the bone on tan construction paper.

Use with "Shamrock Necklaces" on page 103 and "St. Patrick's Day Mobiles" on page 102.

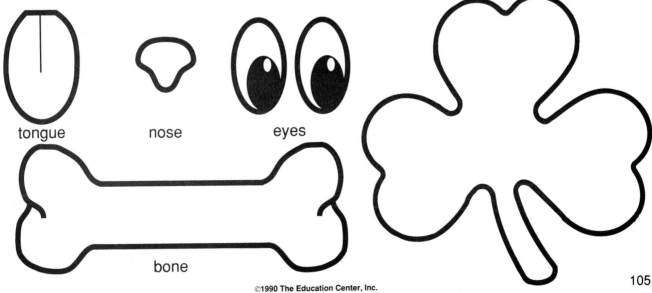

tongue   nose   eyes

bone

©1990 The Education Center, Inc.

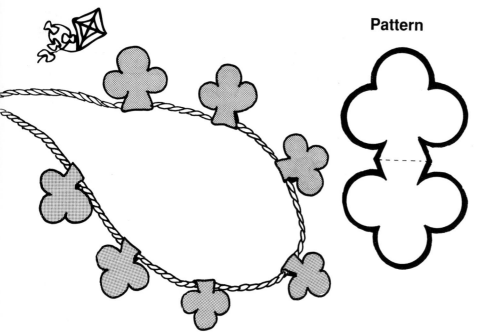

Pattern

Shamrock Jewelry

Gosh and begorra, celebrate St. Patrick's Day with the wearin' of the green! Duplicate the pattern given on green construction paper. Have each child cut a piece of green yarn the length of his desired necklace, bracelet, headband, or belt. The student then cuts out each shamrock, folds it on the dotted line, and glues it over the yarn. Have students decorate their shamrocks, if desired, before decking themselves in Irish green!

Lucky Leprechaun Greetings

Catch these lucky leprechauns to add an Irish flair just in time for your St. Patrick's Day festivities.

Materials Needed:
12" x 18" sheets of green construction paper
assorted construction paper
small paper plates or manila art paper
scissors
glue
crayons

Instructions:
1. Fold a 12" x 18" piece of green construction paper in half along the length; then fold it along the breadth twice as shown.
2. After unfolding the paper, cut off the lower left and right rectangles (as shown), using the fold lines as a guide. Keep the rectangles.
3. To form the leprechaun's jacket, fold the two outermost rectangles inward. Make lapels for the jacket by folding diagonally as shown.
4. To make the leprechaun's pants, cut on lower portion of the middle fold line. Turn up the bottom of each pant's leg for a cuff and glue.
5. For sleeves, glue the rectangles (from Step 2) behind the jacket area. Turn up the sleeve bottoms for cuffs and glue.
6. On a small-size paper plate (or a six-inch manila circle), glue construction paper facial features, a beard, ears, and a hat. Attach the head to the leprechaun's torso along with construction paper hands, shoes, buttons, and several shamrocks. Add crayon details if desired.
7. Write a St. Patrick's Day greeting inside the leprechaun's jacket.

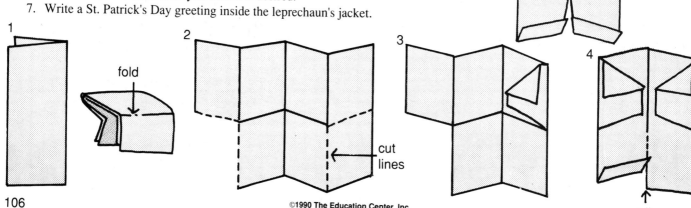

©1990 The Education Center, Inc.

Bunny Bag

This bunny bag begins with a small, white paper sack. Flatten the sack; then cut it to make the ear and head shape as shown. Add construction paper features and fill with cellophane grass and Easter treats!

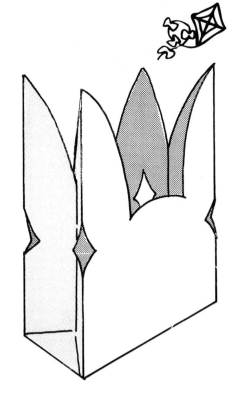

Elegant Easter Eggs

There's no doubt that this Easter decoration will be a favorite among your students! Generously wrap an inflated balloon with crochet thread, crossing the thread continuously. Pour liquid starch over the wrapped balloon until the thread is saturated. Dry the balloon overnight on top of an opened egg carton or over a small bowl. Turn the balloon over in the morning to complete drying. When the thread has completely dried, pop the balloon. Cut a hole in the balloon shape as shown. Add lace, rickrack, or other decorations around the open edge. Fill the egg with Easter grass and other holiday surprises.

Easter Nests

This recipe makes perfect nests for Easter chicks! Melt 1/2 cup of butter in a saucepan. Add 1 cup of brown sugar. Boil and stir for one minute. Add a 3-ounce can of chow mein noodles. Put the mixture in 12 paper baking cups in a muffin tin. Use your thumb to press noodles into a nest shape while still warm. *Do not bake.* Allow nests to cool. Give jelly beans to children to place in the centers of their nests.

©1990 The Education Center, Inc.

Easter Baskets

This colorful Easter basket art is just the trick for your youngsters. Provide brown or black, construction paper strips with one strip being longer than the others for a handle. Have each student glue some strips horizontally and some vertically on a pastel sheet of construction paper before gluing the longer strip on for a handle. Instruct students to shake a different color of dry tempera paint with cotton balls in each paper lunch bag. The children then glue the cotton balls on for Easter eggs. Provide cellophane grass to be glued on as the finishing touch.

Bunnies On Stage

It's time to get hoppin', and these puppet bunnies may be just the thing to put some bounce into your art time. On the back of a paper plate, glue on construction paper facial features and add details with markers. Glue construction paper ears to the rim of the other side of the plate. Staple or glue a second plate to the back of the original one, leaving an opening which is large enough to accommodate your hand. Let the bunny show begin!

Mosaic Easter Eggs

The Easter bunny may be fooled by these torn-paper Easter eggs which, from a distance, appear to be made from crushed eggshells! Duplicate an egg pattern onto white construction paper. Have students draw designs on their egg shapes, then fill the patterns by gluing torn bits of construction paper onto the egg shapes. These colorful eggs make a striking bulletin board when displayed with a lower border of construction paper grass and bunny cutouts.

108

©1990 The Education Center, Inc.

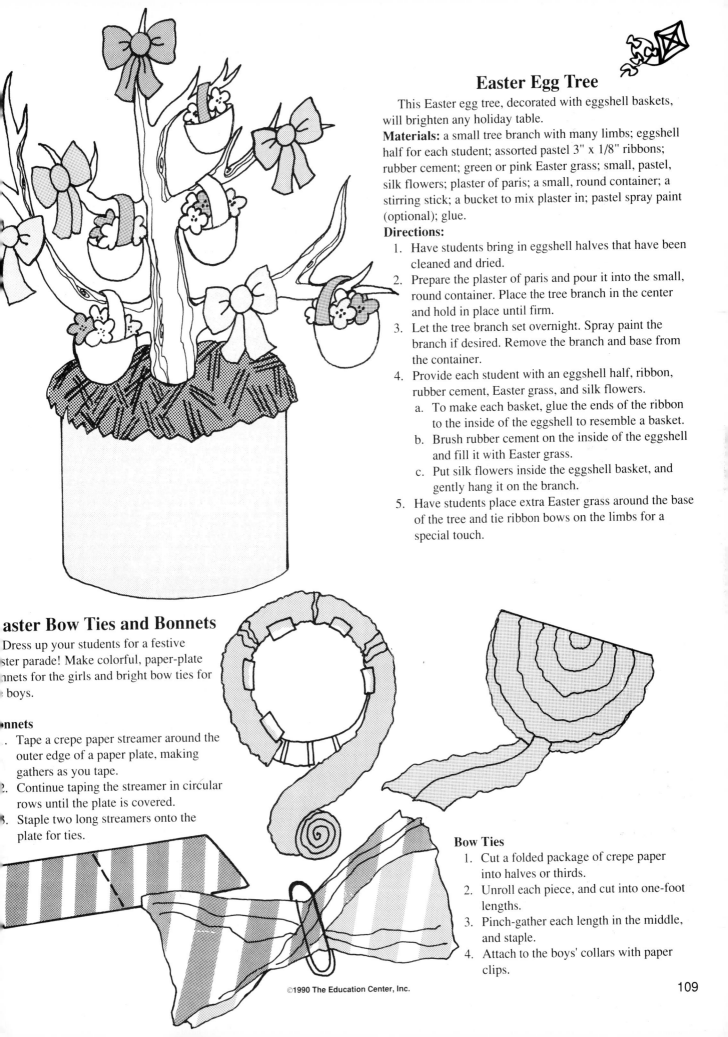

Easter Egg Tree

This Easter egg tree, decorated with eggshell baskets, will brighten any holiday table.

Materials: a small tree branch with many limbs; eggshell half for each student; assorted pastel 3" x 1/8" ribbons; rubber cement; green or pink Easter grass; small, pastel, silk flowers; plaster of paris; a small, round container; a stirring stick; a bucket to mix plaster in; pastel spray paint (optional); glue.

Directions:

1. Have students bring in eggshell halves that have been cleaned and dried.
2. Prepare the plaster of paris and pour it into the small, round container. Place the tree branch in the center and hold in place until firm.
3. Let the tree branch set overnight. Spray paint the branch if desired. Remove the branch and base from the container.
4. Provide each student with an eggshell half, ribbon, rubber cement, Easter grass, and silk flowers.
   a. To make each basket, glue the ends of the ribbon to the inside of the eggshell to resemble a basket.
   b. Brush rubber cement on the inside of the eggshell and fill it with Easter grass.
   c. Put silk flowers inside the eggshell basket, and gently hang it on the branch.
5. Have students place extra Easter grass around the base of the tree and tie ribbon bows on the limbs for a special touch.

aster Bow Ties and Bonnets

Dress up your students for a festive
ster parade! Make colorful, paper-plate
nnets for the girls and bright bow ties for
 boys.

nnets

. Tape a crepe paper streamer around the outer edge of a paper plate, making gathers as you tape.
. Continue taping the streamer in circular rows until the plate is covered.
. Staple two long streamers onto the plate for ties.

Bow Ties

1. Cut a folded package of crepe paper into halves or thirds.
2. Unroll each piece, and cut into one-foot lengths.
3. Pinch-gather each length in the middle, and staple.
4. Attach to the boys' collars with paper clips.

©1990 The Education Center, Inc.

Easter Rabbit Magnet

Paint a clothespin white; then attach wiggle eyes and small, pink and white pom-poms for the nose. Paint on black whiskers and eyelashes, and pink ears. Glue a magnet on the back for a bunny that's cute as well as practical!

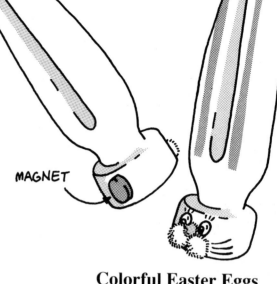

MAGNET

HAPPY EASTER!

Colorful Easter Eggs

Your students are sure to enjoy making these Easter egg designs. Have each student cut a length of waxed paper and fold it in half, sandwiching in multicolored crayon shavings. Using a warm, foil-covered iron, press or have students press the waxed paper to melt the crayon shavings. After the waxed paper has cooled, have each student cut it into an egg shape. Mount the egg cutouts on construction paper to decorate student-made greeting cards or for an Easter display.

Far-out Egg Heads

You may be surprised by the results when you turn your students loose on this creative assignment. Duplicate an egg pattern onto white construction paper. Provide glue, scissors, construction paper scraps, tissue paper, yarn, foil, fabric, sequins, and whatever miscellaneous craft supplies you have on hand. After displaying several samples to get your students started, have them use the supplies to create the egg-headed personalities of their choice.

Follow up this activity by having students write brief biographies or adventure stories in which their eggs play the leading roles.

©1990 The Education Center, Inc.

Rabbit Basket

Have students save and bring in green, plastic soft drink bottles. Remove the bottom piece of each bottle. (Some pieces can simply be pulled off; others may need to be cut off using an X-acto knife or razor blade.) For each basket, you'll need a large white pom-pom for the rabbit face, wiggle eyes, two or three black pipe cleaners, and a pink pom-pom for a nose. Glue the eyes and nose to the white pom-pom. Cut the pipe cleaners in half; then glue them to the face for whiskers. Using a pattern, cut four ears from pink gingham material or construction paper. For each ear, place a pipe cleaner between the two ear cutouts for support and glue them together. To assemble, glue the rabbit face and ears to the bottle bottom and add a white cotton ball tail. Fill the basket with Easter grass and treats.

Giant Classroom Egg

Draw a huge Easter egg on white bulletin board paper for this classroom mural. Divide it into as many sections as there are students in your class. Have each child paint a scene or design in his section. The finished product will resemble a quilt. Adapt this idea by using other holiday shapes.

©1990 The Education Center, Inc.

Easter Bunny

Hatch a cottony Easter bunny! Cut out and decorate an Easter egg from white paper. Then cut the egg in half along a zigzag line. Glue one half of the egg on the top half of a piece of art paper. Glue cotton balls to the paper to make the top half of a bunny. Glue the second half of the egg in place, slipping it over the bunny. Add construction paper features to the bunny's face.

Glistening Easter Eggs

Break away from the ordinary—consider the "egg-ceptional." This glistening egg project is guaranteed to delight the Easter bunny himself. Mix sweetened condensed milk and food coloring to create several colors of "paint." Paint this mixture onto giant eggs cut from 12" x 18" sheets of construction paper. When dry, these eggs may be displayed together for a beautiful, glistening effect.

Cotton Ball Bunnies

Hang Easter bunny ornaments from your egg tree this year. Cut rabbit ears, eyes, nose, and mouth from construction paper, and glue to a large cotton ball. To make the egg shape, dip colorful yarn in glue which has been thinned with water. Wrap the yarn around a balloon, leaving an opening in front as shown. Before hanging the balloon up to dry, sprinkle it with transparent glitter if desired. When the yarn is dry, pop the balloon. Fill with colored Easter grass, and put the cotton ball bunny inside.

©1990 The Education Center, Inc.

Eggshell Art

Dyed eggshells make beautiful mosaic designs. Have students save white and brown eggshells over several weeks' time, or ask a local restaurant that serves breakfast to save shells for you. You will need shells from about 500 eggs for 50 students. Have students wash eggshells, and let them dry. Place shells in a plastic garbage bag and crush them. Children enjoy stepping on the shells they have collected for this group effort!

Use either egg-coloring dyes or tempera paint to dye batches of the eggshells in large coffee cans. Lay colored shells on paper towel–lined trays or plates to dry. Have each student draw a picture or design on mat board. Children then glue colored shells to fill in their designs. Display mosaic designs by standing them on the chalk tray.

Posy Planters

A pretty planter makes a great Mother's Day gift.

Materials:

ter's clay
lling pin
egg-shaped, oaktag pattern
nife
wl of water

small pieces of paper
pencil
glaze
potting soil and a small
    plant (or Styrofoam and
    artificial greenery)

Instructions for students:

. Roll the clay flat using a rolling pin.
. Place the oaktag pattern on the clay and use the knife to cut around it. Repeat this process; then cut the second egg-shaped piece of clay in half horizontally.
. Position the half piece atop the egg-shaped clay. Fuse the edges of the clay pieces with wet fingers, leaving the top open. Press a design into the clay edges—similar to a fluted piecrust.
. Stuff small pieces of paper into the opening to hold the planter open while the clay dries.
. Use a pencil to make a hole near the top of the planter for hanging.
. Allow clay to dry. Remove the paper. Fire in a kiln. (If there's not a kiln available at your school, ask to use one at a local high school.) Glaze and fire again.
. Plant a small plant in the bowl of the planter. Or put some Styrofoam in the planter, and insert artificial greenery.

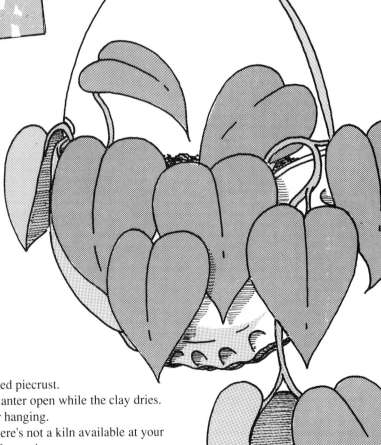

©1990 The Education Center, Inc.

Mother's Day Magnet

These refrigerator magnets are lovely Mother's Day gifts. You will need wooden thread spools (from craft stores), small dried flowers, glue, yarn or ribbon, and magnetic tape for this project. Have the spools cut in half as shown. Students glue flowers in the grooves on the backs of the spools and tie with yarn or ribbon. Attach a magnet strip to the back of each spool.

Spool cut
in half

Pop Art

Add a little "pop" to your art with these pop-up pictures. Fold a lightweight paper plate in half; then unfold. Draw and color a background scene inside the paper plate; then refold the plate. Cut two identical slits intersecting the fold of the plate (approximately one-half inch apart) to create each pop-up tab. When all tabs have been cut, open the plate and fold the tabs to the inside. Attach a construction paper figure to each tab to complete the picture.

To convert your pop art into a Mother's Day card, attach construction paper to the back of the plate and decorate as shown.

Happy Mother's Day!

I love you!

What's Cookin': Parsley Potatoes

Mom's Recipe Holder

Here's the recipe for a lovely Mother's Day gift. For each recipe holder you will need a three-inch-square block of wood, wood stain, a paintbrush, aerosol acrylic sealer, tempera paint, a spring-type clothespin, glue, and a recipe card. Stain the clothespin and block of wood, and allow to dry. Seal with acrylic sealer. When dry, paint a design on one side of the wooden block. Glue the clothespin to the opposite side. Clip a recipe card in the clothespin, and this recipe holder is ready to adorn the countertop of a lucky mom.

©1990 The Education Center, Inc.

did

Mother's Teakettle

This kettle card whistles a merry message for Mother's
[Da]y. Use the pattern to make two paper kettles for each
[stu]dent. Students insert tea bags between their kettles, and
[stap]le them at the top. Have each child decorate the front
[of th]is "cover" kettle and write this message inside.

Here's a gift for Mother's Day:
I'll try my best in every way.
But when you get upset with me,
Relax and have a pot of tea!

Love,

inside of card

Pattern

©1990 The Education Center, Inc.

Stir-Stick Wall Decorations

Stir up colorful wall decorations with wooden stir sticks. Stain the stick and let it dry. Glue on dried beans, rice, peas, popcorn, or sunflower seeds to make a picture or design. Alphabet noodles are great for writing creative messages. Tie a pretty ribbon on the stick and send it home for Mother's Day.

Gumdrop Flower Corsage

Mom can wear, and then munch on, this Mother's Day gift. Cut out a four-inch circle from poster board and glue it to a five-inch doily. To make the flowers, push gumdrops onto the ends of green pipe cleaners. Push several small, tissue paper pieces up each pipe cleaner and around the gumdrop. Insert finished flowers in the center of the doily and add a bow to their stems for a finishing touch.

Mother's Day Bouquet

A basket of job-labeled flowers will let Mom choose a gift seven days a week. Staple or glue an eight-inch construction paper square into a cone shape. Attach a 1/2" x 6" paper handle. Each child prints a job he would like to do for Mom on each of seven 7-inch paper stems. He then attaches a crumpled tissue paper blossom to each.

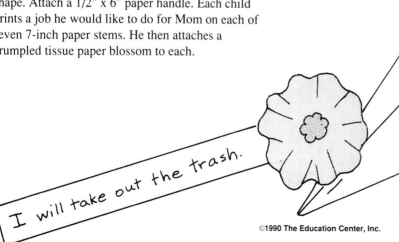

116

©1990 The Education Center, Inc.

A Mother's Day Surprise

Warm the hearts of your students' mothers and grandmothers with these unique gifts! Duplicate student copies of the pattern below. Color, cut out, and mount the pattern onto the front of a 9" x 12" folded construction paper card. Copy, then glue, the poem inside the card. With student assistance, mix one recipe of bath salts for every 12 students. Using double-sided tape, attach a Ziploc bag containing 1/4 cup of bath salts inside each card. As a finishing touch, have students wrap cards in tissue paper and attach completed gift tags made from wallpaper scraps.

Bath Salts Recipe

3 cups Epsom salts	1 tablespoon glycerin
perfume	two drops food coloring

Place Epsom salts in a glass or metal container. Combine glycerin and food coloring. Add perfume to make a fragrant mixture; then add to Epsom salts. Stir thoroughly.

Pattern

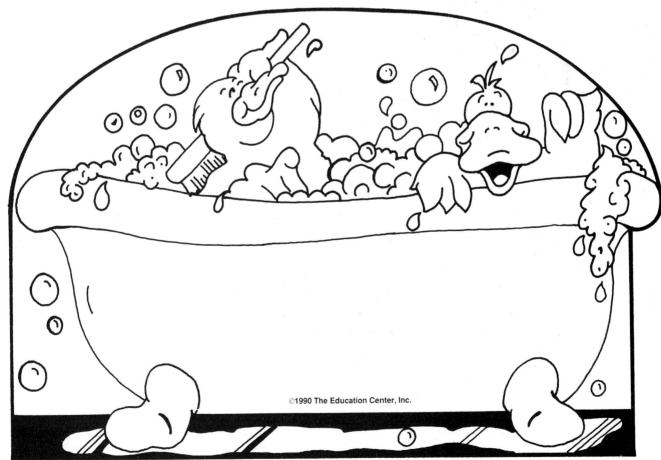

©1990 The Education Center, Inc.

©1990 The Education Center, Inc.

117

Mother's Day Sachets

Create these three-dimensional sachets to freshen up any drawer or room. Mom will love it!

Materials:
heart patterns (page 79)
glue
scissors
perfume
yarn
felt
cotton balls
fabric
ribbon or lace

Directions:
1. Trace a heart shape onto two pieces of felt.
2. Cut the center out of one felt heart to make a window.
3. Put a few drops of perfume on a cotton ball. Glue the cotton to the center of the whole heart.
4. Glue a piece of fabric over the cotton.
5. Position a yarn loop between the felt hearts, and glue the two hearts together.
6. Add ribbon or lace for decorations.
7. Give it to your mother to hang in her closet.

1.

2. 3.

4. 5.

6.

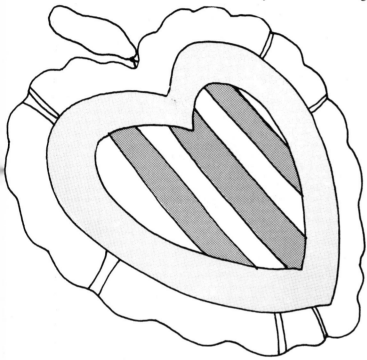

Baby Jar Gifts

Here's a creative project that students may give as Mother's Day gifts. For each child, supply a clean, baby-food jar with a lid. (Substitute small, plastic containers from beverage mixes or frosting if your students are prohibited from carrying glass containers on the bus.) Spray-paint the lids with nontoxic paint, if desired. Have each student select from recent artwork a small drawing, section of a painting, or finger-painting sample. Trim it to fit the side of the jar. Assist student in "painting" Modge Podge™ on the exterior of the jar excluding rim and bottom. Help student place artwork on the Modge Podge. Brush over the artwork with Modge Podge. Have student sprinkle the entire jar with clear or frosted glitter. When jars are dry, have students fill with candy or bath salts for gift giving. Carefully pack each jar in several layers of newspaper and caution each student about breakage.

©1990 The Education Center, Inc.

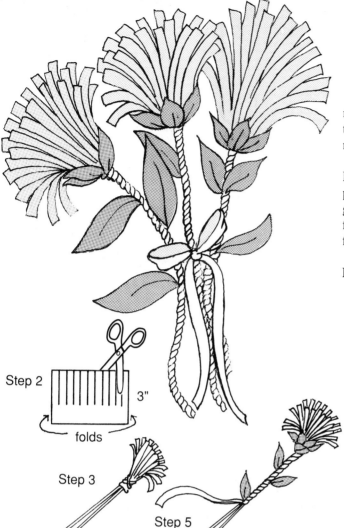

Bouquets For Mothers

Student-made flower bouquets are lovely thank-yous for room mothers or Mother's Day gifts. You'll find that it's time-consuming for students to make these flowers, but the results are gifts your students will be proud to give.

Materials needed:

pink, red, or lavender crepe paper   scissors
green crepe paper   ribbon
floral wire   perfume
floral tape

Instructions:

1. Cutting through several thicknesses of green crepe paper, cut out leaf shapes.
2. Cut a three-inch-wide strip from folded red, pink, or lavender crepe paper and fringe it.
3. After unfolding the strip, gather unfringed side and secure with floral wire.
4. Wrap the wire with floral tape.
5. Wrapping your way down the "stem," insert leaf cutouts at intervals.
6. Spray finished flowers with perfume, and tie several together with a matching ribbon.

Mother's Day Card

Follow the steps shown to make a tulip-shaped card from a piece of 9" x 12" construction paper. After completing the card, each child decorates with paint or chalk and writes a message inside.

1. Fold on dotted lines so that the ends meet in the center.

2. Fold backwards on dotted center line.

3. Cut on dotted lines.

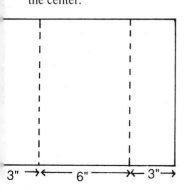

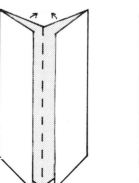

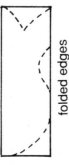

folded edges

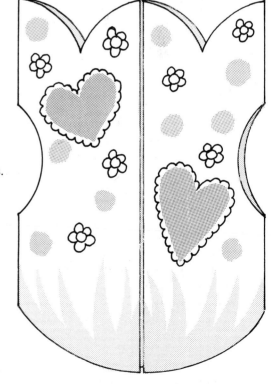

Finished card

©1990 The Education Center, Inc.

119

Covered Flowerpots

Choose one of these flowerpot projects as a Mother's Day gift or for a spring planting project. Individual clay pots are needed, but green thumbs are not required!

Simulated Cork: (*Materials*—masking tape, any type of brown shoe polish) Cover the pot completely with two-inch strips of masking tape. Polish the pot surface with shoe polish and allow to dry. The result is corklike!

Rug Yarn: (*Materials*—glue, paintbrush, rug yarn) Brush glue over the first inch of the pot, starting from the bottom edge. Wrap the rug yarn around the bottom edge of the pot. Continue wrapping upwards, keeping the yarn wraps very close together. Brush on additional glue as needed and continue wrapping until the entire pot is covered. Use contrasting colors of rug yarn to glue additional shapes or designs on top of the yarn surface if desired.

Calico: (*Materials*—glue, paintbrush, fabric scraps, pinking shears) Use pinking shears to cut fabric scraps into two- and three-inch squares. Brush squares with glue and apply to pot. Overlap squares for added texture. Cover the entire pot.

Protect dry, completed pots with a coat of spray-on, clear shellac or polyurethane.

Tea For "Tea-rrific" Moms

Students will enjoy surprising Moms on Mother's Day. To make a greeting card, fold a sheet of construction paper in half. Label the card as shown. Trace the teacup pattern on page 122 on wallpaper or construction paper, and cut out. Fold and glue the sides, but not the top where you insert tea bags. Glue the teacup inside the card and fill with Mom's favorite tea bags!

©1990 The Education Center, Inc.

Mom's Coupon Holder

Make a handy coupon holder for Mom. Cut construction paper or wallpaper into an eight-inch square and fold in half. Punch holes along three sides and lace with yarn.

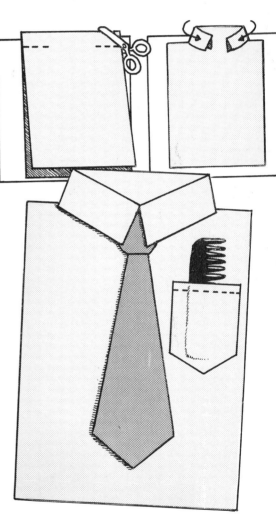

Father's Day Greeting

Convert construction paper into a dress shirt as a special greeting for Dad on his day! Fold a sheet of 18" x 6" construction paper in half. About 1 1/2 inches below the fold, cut slits and fold as shown to make a collar. Glue the collar in place. Onto the shirt, glue the sides and bottom only of a 2 1/2-inch-deep construction paper pocket. Then glue on a tie (pattern on page 122). Add details with a marker or crayon. Slip an inexpensive, black, pocket-size comb into the shirt pocket. Open the folded card, and write a special message for Dad inside.

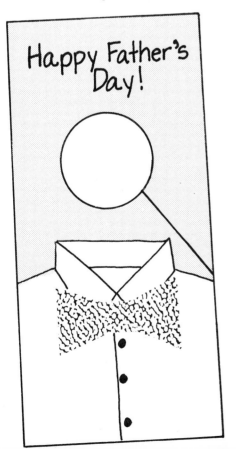

Door Messages For Dads

Youngsters will enjoy surprising their dads with festive Father's Day door hangers. You will need a 4 1/2" x 12" sheet of construction paper for each child, construction paper scraps, glitter, scissors, glue, and black markers. Have each student fold his construction paper lengthwise and cut a half-circle on the fold about three inches from the top. After unfolding the paper, each student makes a diagonal cut ending at the circular cutout as shown. Students decorate door hangers as desired using construction paper scraps, glitter, glue, and markers.

©1990 The Education Center, Inc.

121

Use with "Father's Day Greeting" on page 121 and "Dad's Pad" on page 123.

Use with "Tea For 'Tea-rrific' Mom" on page 120.

←fold line

©1990 The Education Center, Inc.

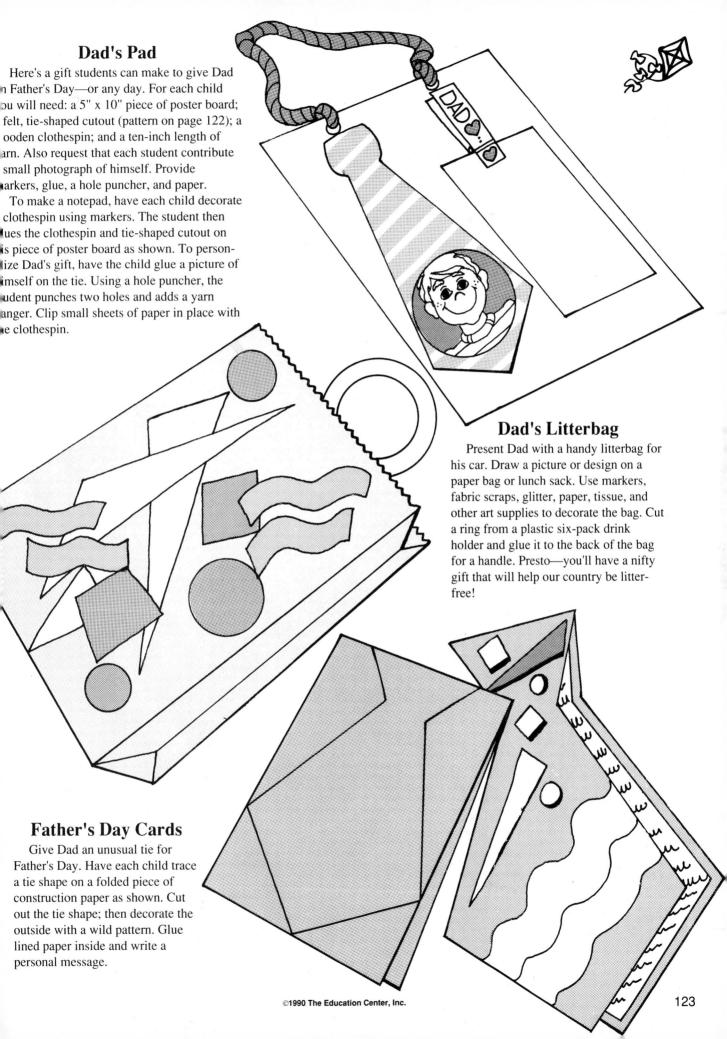

Dad's Pad

Here's a gift students can make to give Dad on Father's Day—or any day. For each child you will need: a 5" x 10" piece of poster board; a felt, tie-shaped cutout (pattern on page 122); a wooden clothespin; and a ten-inch length of yarn. Also request that each student contribute a small photograph of himself. Provide markers, glue, a hole puncher, and paper.

To make a notepad, have each child decorate a clothespin using markers. The student then glues the clothespin and tie-shaped cutout on his piece of poster board as shown. To personalize Dad's gift, have the child glue a picture of himself on the tie. Using a hole puncher, the student punches two holes and adds a yarn hanger. Clip small sheets of paper in place with the clothespin.

Dad's Litterbag

Present Dad with a handy litterbag for his car. Draw a picture or design on a paper bag or lunch sack. Use markers, fabric scraps, glitter, paper, tissue, and other art supplies to decorate the bag. Cut a ring from a plastic six-pack drink holder and glue it to the back of the bag for a handle. Presto—you'll have a nifty gift that will help our country be litter-free!

Father's Day Cards

Give Dad an unusual tie for Father's Day. Have each child trace a tie shape on a folded piece of construction paper as shown. Cut out the tie shape; then decorate the outside with a wild pattern. Glue lined paper inside and write a personal message.

©1990 The Education Center, Inc.

Many Thanks!

Surprise and thank each of your parent volunteers with a special thank-you bookle Each student traces his hand onto a 9" x 6 sheet of white construction paper, then writes a thank-you note inside his outline. Using different-colored markers or crayon the student continues to draw around his outline until he reaches the edge of his paper, creating a rainbow effect. Prepare a tagboard cover entitled "Thanks For The Helping Hand, [parent name]!" Punch hol in the cover and the construction paper pages. Tie the booklet together with satin ribbon. Be sure to include your own personalized thank-you in each booklet.

Patchwork Memories

Students color 8" muslin squares for a memorable end-of-the-year project. Have each child use crayons to draw something that you can remember him by. When all squares are completed, sew strips of fabric between them to resemble a quilt. The children will love seeing it displayed on the wall!

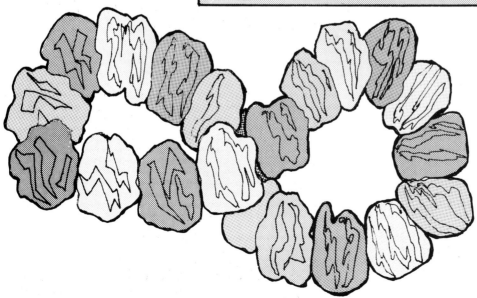

Last-Day Leis

Create unique tissue paper leis as an end of-the-year art project. Students may keep their leis or present them to others who hav helped to make their year more pleasant. Roll four-inch squares of brightly colored tissue paper into small balls. Using a needl and thread, make several passes through a button and string the tissue paper balls together. When a desired length is reached connect the ends of the lei by restringing th button, then knotting and tying the thread. Aloha!

©1990 The Education Center, Inc.

Anytime

Class Mosaic

This art project will keep early finishers busy. Trace or draw a large picture on poster board or paper. Mount on an easel or bulletin board. Provide glue and small squares of colored tissue paper. During their free time, have small groups of children fill in the picture with the tissue paper squares. (You may wish to glue one piece of tissue in each section of the picture to guide younger students.) Use this technique to create decorations for a unit theme or to celebrate the season.

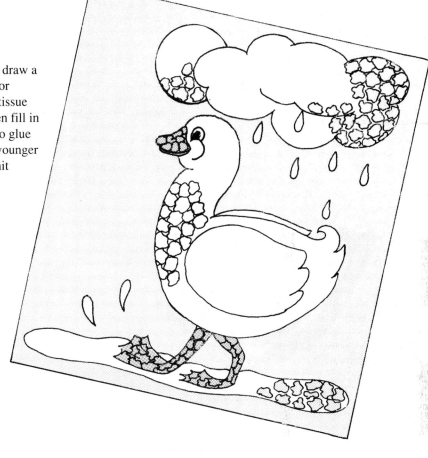

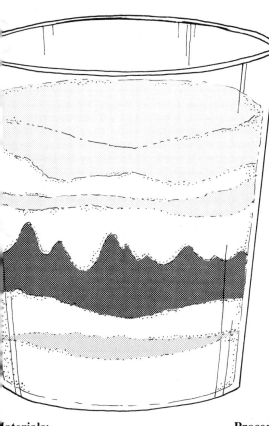

Sand Scene

Peaks and valleys add new dimensions to ordinary sand art. After completing your sand scene, insert a thin wire carefully between the layers of sand and the edge of the container, and pull it out vertically.

Materials:
sand
large plastic bowls
liquid tempera paint
clear plastic cups or small glass bottles
tablespoons
thin wire

Procedure:

1. Fill plastic bowls 2/3 full of sand.
2. Add 1 to 2 tablespoons of liquid tempera paint to the sand. Stir until well mixed. (The intensity of the color depends on the quantity of tempera paint you use.) You may want to leave some sand uncolored or use salt.
3. Let the colored sand dry overnight. Do *not* seal sand containers until the sand is dry.
4. Layer the sand in clear containers to make colorful scenes.
5. Use wire inserted in the jar to make peaks and valleys.
6. *Don't* tilt or shake the containers after you're finished.

©1990 The Education Center, Inc.

Glue Pictures

Here's a simple activity that students will stick with until they're finished! After each child lightly sketches a design on black construction paper, have him squeeze liquid glue onto the lines. When the glue dries into a clear design, the student colors in each section with brightly colored chalk. Spray with a fixative before displaying.

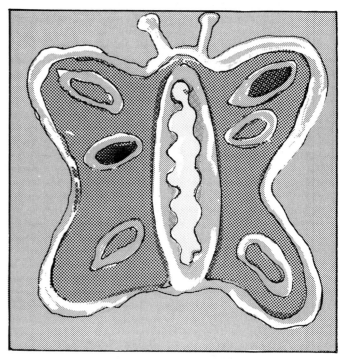

Sun Catchers

With this art project, your students can mix colors. Provide each child with a clear, plastic cup that has two holes punched in the bottom. Children thread yarn through the holes to make hangers for their sun catchers. Have students paint thinned glue all over the cups before covering cup surfaces with overlapping squares of red, blue, and yellow cellophane or tissue paper. As the sun catchers hang in a sunny location, children can observe for themselves the creation of secondary colors.

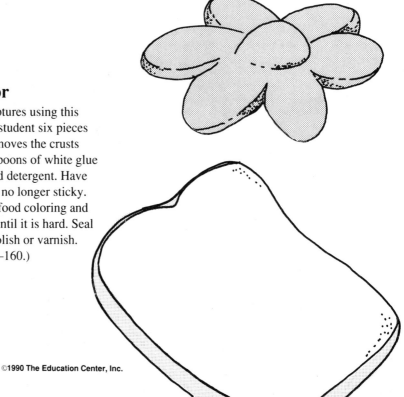

Be A Sculptor

Fill your room with creative sculptures using this easy-to-make bread clay. Give each student six pieces of plain white bread. The student removes the crusts and kneads the bread with six tablespoons of white glue combined with 1/2 teaspoon of liquid detergent. Have students knead the mixture until it is no longer sticky. Then have them tint the "clay" with food coloring and shape it. Let the clay dry overnight until it is hard. Seal your clay creations with clear nail polish or varnish. (For more art recipes, see pages 158–160.)

©1990 The Education Center, Inc.

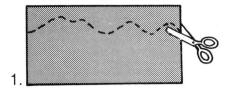

1.

2.

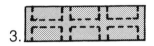

3.

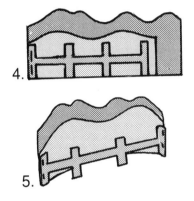

4.

5.

Cut Paper Scenes

With colorful construction paper and a pair of scissors, your students can create dramatic, three-dimensional scenes.

Procedure:

1. Cut out some mountains from a 6" x 12" blue or purple piece of paper.
2. Cut out some rolling hills from a 5" x 9" green piece of paper.
3. Cut out a fence from a 2" x 7" brown piece of paper.
4. Lay the three pieces atop one another as shown and staple together at one end.
5. Now pull the other ends of the three pieces together and staple to make your scene three-dimensional.
6. Cut out and glue paper trees, horses, cows, people, houses, or anything else you want to add to the scene.

6.

BB Games

Turn a mayonnaise or peanut butter jar lid into a fun game! Trace und the jar lid on tagboard and cut out the circle. Decorate the cle, keeping in mind that three or four holes will be punched out of Punch out the holes with a hole punch. Spray paint the jar lid. When , glue the circle into the lid. Add the same number of BBs as holes iched; then cover the lid with clear plastic or plastic wrap. Secure plastic tightly with a rubber band. Glue ribbon around the edge of jar lid, covering the rubber band. When the glue is dry, trim off the ess plastic. Students try to shake the BBs into the holes—what fun!

©1990 The Education Center, Inc.

Sunshine Quilt

Spread a little sunshine to a child who is sick for an extended period. Give each student a piece of construction paper folded in fourths. Each child traces over the folds and makes crayon "stitches" on the lines and around the edges. He draws simple pictures in the boxes to illustrate friendship, happy thoughts, or best wishes. Then he writes and signs a message on the back. Tape all of the papers together to make one large quilt, or punch holes around the edges and lace them together. Send the "quilt" home in a decorated basket.

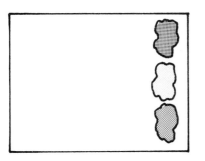

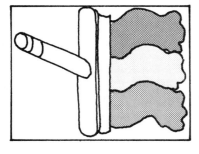

Squeegee Art

Create unique works of art with a squeegee (window washer), food coloring, and art paper. Have each student drop small puddles of food coloring close together along one edge of his paper. Using the squeegee, the student carefully pulls the colors across his paper. Interesting designs are created when the squeegee is pulled in curving lines across the paper. After the papers have dried, encourage students to cut the colored pages into flowers, Easter eggs, and other creative shapes.

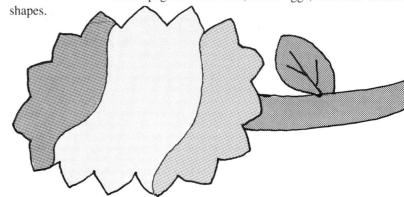

Personalized Pictures

Use these name pictures to fill extra class minutes or for an easy art lesson. Students write their names on *thin* paper folded in half. Have students turn their papers over and trace their names backwards on the other side. Students unfold the papers and decorate with crayons, markers, or paint.

©1990 The Education Center, Inc.

Rainbow Cutouts

Tie a cut-and-paste activity to a cheerful lesson on graduated shades of colors. Provide many colors of construction paper cut into long, narrow strips. Display and discuss how to arrange these colors from darker to lighter hues. Give each student a piece of oaktag. Have the student glue the colored strips next to one another on the oaktag. After the glue has dried, the student draws a faint pencil outline of a shape on the strips. He cuts out the shape and mounts it on a piece of construction paper or hangs it from the ceiling.

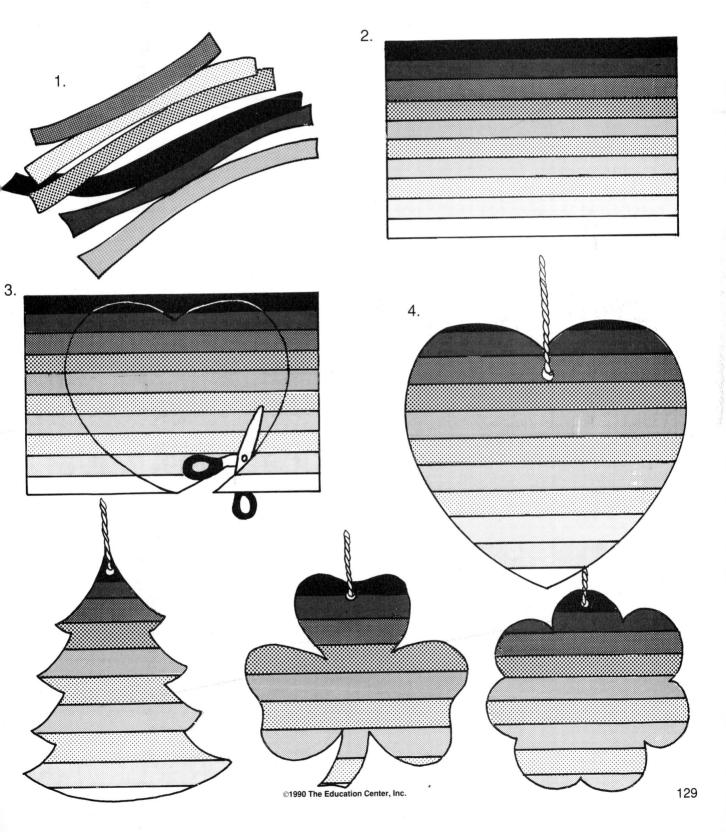

©1990 The Education Center, Inc.

129

Marbleized Art

Here is an art activity students will enjoy as they marbleize barrettes, hair clips, plastic planters, paper bags, or other items. You will need a bucket of water, spray paint in desired colors, art aprons or shirts, newsprint for drying artwork, and plastic or paper items to marbleize.

Each student selects an item to marbleize and a color of paint. The student sprays the paint onto the water. Next he dips the item in the water, pulls it out, and lays it on newsprint to dry. Be sure to spray the water as needed, use clean water for different colors, and complete the project in a well ventilated area.

Gum Balls Galore

Those brown, prickly balls that fall from sweet gum trees can be converted into unique art projects. For a gum ball spider, glue eight, black, four-inch pipe cleaner sections into indentations. Add wiggle eyes to complete these creepy crawlers. Tie monofilament line to the gum ball's stem, and your spider can be suspended from bulletin board tops, door moldings, or light fixtures.

Have your students exercise their creativity by using gum balls and miscellaneous craft supplies to create other unique characters. There's no limit to the fun you can have with these critters.

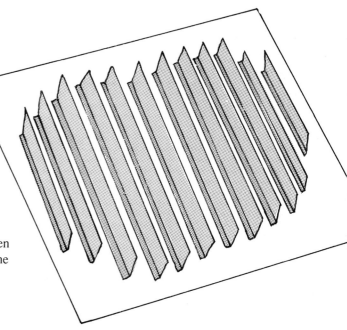

Strip Pictures

Convert your favorite designs into dynamic dimensional artwork with this cut-and-fold-and-glue method. For "apple-icious" September art, trace a large apple shape onto red construction paper and cut out. Then cut vertically into approximately one-inch-wide strips. In turn, fold each strip vertically approximately one-quarter inch from its right side. Glue along folded edges and attach to white art paper, leaving gaps between strips. As art enthusiasts stroll by these creations, they'll find the view changes with each step.

©1990 The Education Center, Inc.

Three-Dimensional Designs

Cut narrow strips of paper from different colors of construction paper. Wrap some strips around a pencil to form curls. Bend others into accordion-style pleats. Glue some strips into circles. Fringe the edges of others. Be creative—think of other ways to turn a strip into something different! When finished, glue the strips on a large sheet of black construction paper to make an interesting, colorful design.

It's Raining, It's Pouring!

A cold, rainy day is the perfect time for students to create their own wet weather scenes. Have each student draw a picture of a rainstorm scene, coloring it with crayons. To add realistic "raindrops," have the child make short slashes on his paper with a blue or purple, nonpermanent marker. Fill a sink or bucket with water. Instruct each student to dip his picture in the water, making sure the rain "falls" in a downward direction. After drying, display these pictures on a bulletin board or hang them on a clothesline suspended across the classroom.

Paper Towel Art

Instead of providing paper towels for cleanup after art, turn them into art! Using markers, children color in the printed designs on kitchen paper towels. Place a sheet of newsprint under each towel before coloring. The bleeding effect of the markers results in a unique finished product.

Sparkling Treasures

Treasures from your nature walks will sparkle when they're preserved with this method. Place flowers (or leaves) between paper towels and press in a heavy book for about two weeks. Remove the backing from a piece of frosted, transparent Con-Tact paper; then arrange the flowers in a single layer on the sticky side. Carefully place a second piece of Con-Tact paper over the flowers. Cut two cardboard frames to fit the Con-Tact paper. Staple one frame to the front and one to the back of the Con-Tact paper. Punch a hole at the top and add a string to make a lovely sun catcher.

Projects From Plates

Turn paper plates into some favorite barnyard friends! You can purchase paper plates in every color. But, if the expense is prohibitiv children may paint white plates with tempera paint. The materials an procedures for making a horse are below. Make a few color and shap changes to create a whole barnyard of critters!

Materials Needed To Make A Horse:

large brown paper plate   markers
small brown paper plate   scissors
glue   stapler   black tissue paper strips
two, brown, construction paper triangles (ears)
four, brown, construction paper rectangles (legs)
black construction paper circles or wiggle eyes

Procedure:

1. Staple the paper plates together as shown.
2. Glue triangles (ears) and rectangles (legs) to the backs of the plates.
3. Attach circles or wiggle eyes.
4. Glue on tissue paper strips for mane and tail. Trim the mane to desired length.
5. Add nostrils and hooves with markers.

©1990 The Education Center, Inc.

Clothes Hanger Puppets

Choose favorite nursery rhyme characters to make into puppets. Form wire hangers into ovals. Stretch a nylon stocking over each oval and secure at the handle. Add cutout facial features, details, and hair to the hanger faces. Have children hold puppets in front of their faces as they act out rhymes.

Rag Rug

If your class is studying colonial life or you're looking for a cooperative art project, let students make a rag rug. Cut a large number of fabric strips, approximately 1 1/2" to 2" wide. Have students tie or hand-stitch the strips end to end, making three very long strips. Students then braid the strips together until a desired length is achieved. Coil the braid and have students stitch the rug together. This worthwhile project can be time-consuming, so allow students to work on it during free time throughout the year.

Clip Art

As a class, brainstorm unique ways to use Band-Aids, rubber bands, and paper clips. Then distribute one of each item to each student along with a piece of colored construction paper of his choice. Ask students to create something using the three objects, paper, scissors, crayons, and glue. The rubber band may be cut; the paper clip may be bent. Encourage originality and imagination by stressing that no two pictures or creations should be alike. Be prepared for Band-Aid mustaches, paper-clip bugs, and rubber-band hair!

©1990 The Education Center, Inc.

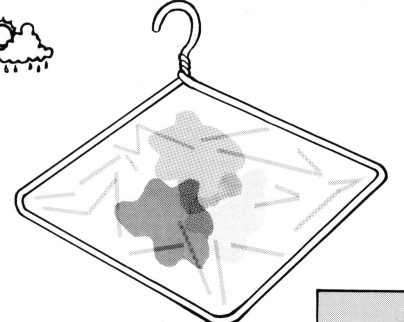

Hang Glows

Spread some sunshine with primary colors. Place a sheet of plastic wrap on each student's desk. Bend a coat hanger in any shape and place it on top of the plastic wrap. Spread watered-down, white glue over the plastic wrap and hanger. Drop primary colors of food coloring over the glue; then place a second sheet of plastic wrap on top of this. As students press colors together, they see how primary colors mix to form secondary colors. Allow designs to dry one day. Trim the edges of the plastic wrap, and hang designs in sunlight.

Mosaic Underwater Scenes

There's nothing fishy about this art project. Making underwater mosaics will give your students an opportunity to be creative. Collect blue construction paper, green tissue paper, glue, beans, macaroni, spaghetti, yarn, pebbles, rice, fish-shaped crackers, and shells for this activity. Have students sketch an underwater scene on blue construction paper. Then have them glue beans, macaroni, rice, and other materials inside the outlines. Green tissue paper seaweed may then be added. Have students complete the effect by gluing on seashells and fish-shaped crackers.

Edible Peanut Butter Clay

Try this recipe for an afternoon of modeling fun and a tasty snack all in one! Mix 2 cups of peanut butter with 1 cup of honey. (Swirl 1 teaspoon of oil in the measuring cup before measuring to avoid sticking.) Add 3 cups of instant dry milk, a little at a time, until stiff. Blend with hands. Refrigerate overnight. The next day, provide each child with a piece of waxed paper and some peanut butter clay. Have students mold their clay into different shapes. When finished, let the students eat their creations. (This recipe makes enough clay for 18 students. For more art recipes, see pages 158–160.)

©1990 The Education Center, Inc.

Potato Monsters

When you create these wrinkled monsters, they continue to grow strange appendages! To make a monster, each child will need a sprouting potato, a metal jar lid, a nail, scraps of tissue paper, glue, a pair of wiggly eyes, and watercolor paints. Without breaking off sprouts, children paint their potatoes and sprouts in contrasting colors. Next, each child drives a nail through his jar lid and covers the lid with tissue paper. After mounting painted potatoes carefully on the nails, students glue on eyes and other materials to create "spuds from space" or Irish gnomes.

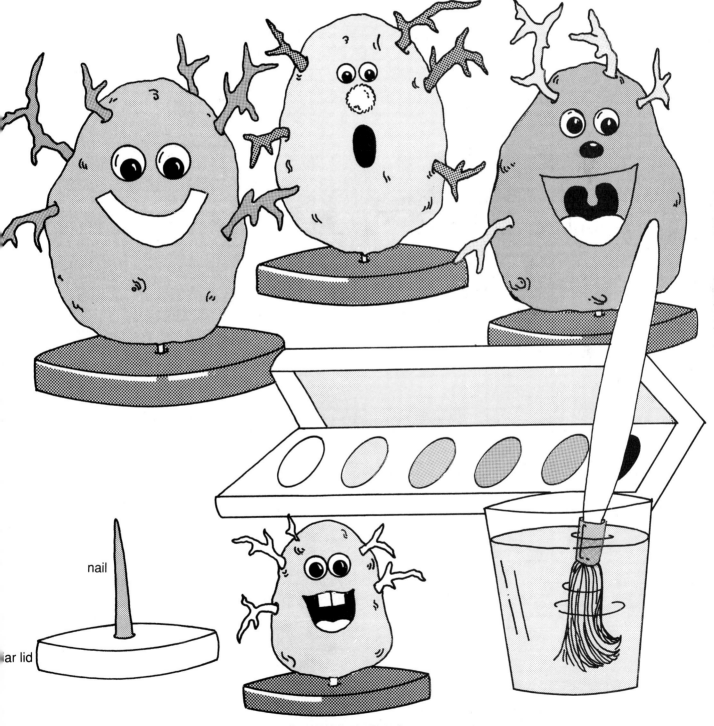

nail

jar lid

©1990 The Education Center, Inc.

Plum Delicious!

Imagine how purple little Jack Horner's hands would have been after eating the plum pie with his fingers! Your students will enjoy having purple fingers for a few minutes, too. Provide purple finger paint, and have students create purple finger-painted papers. After the paintings are dry, have each child trace and cut out a large, brown construction paper circle and a smaller, purple finger-painted circle. Have the child paste the purple circle atop the brown one. Next the student crisscrosses and attaches a brown paper "crust" atop the circles. To finish, have the child trace and cut out his hand from construction paper. The student pastes a purple plum cutout on his thumb and pastes the hand cutout on the pie. My, my what purple pies!

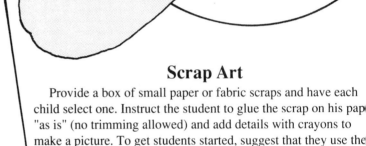

Scrap Art

Provide a box of small paper or fabric scraps and have each child select one. Instruct the student to glue the scrap on his paper "as is" (no trimming allowed) and add details with crayons to make a picture. To get students started, suggest that they use the scraps as common objects: kite, flag, sail, tablecloth, etc.

Watermelon Still Life

What could be more refreshing in the afternoon than a cold watermelon and an art lesson? Bring in a large watermelon for a still life subject. Slice and arrange the watermelon on a red-checkered tablecloth with the knife sticking in the melon. After drawing, enjoy eating the "model" and save some of the seeds. Later, students paint their drawings with watercolors and add some real seeds.

©1990 The Education Center, Inc.

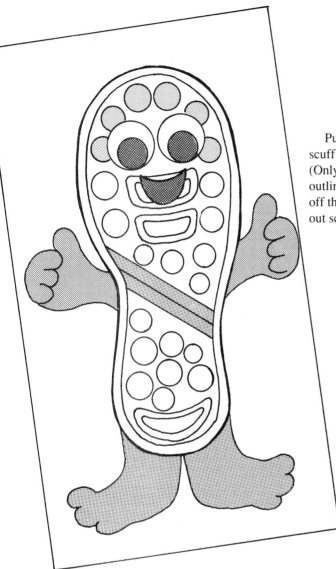

Foot Printing

Put your best foot forward with this fun art project. Have students scuff their sneakers on the floor before stepping on pieces of white paper. (Only sneakers with patterns on the soles will be effective.) Each child outlines the edge and sole design with fine-tipped markers before shaking off the dust from the paper. After coloring the designs, have students cut out scraps of construction paper to glue onto their pictures.

Watercolor And Rubber Cement Batik

Draw a design on a piece of white paper. Plan to use a three-color heme using watercolors. Paint the entire paper with the lightest color d let dry. Cover the parts of the design you want to remain light with thick coat of rubber cement. When dry, paint the entire surface with e medium color and let dry. Then cover the parts you want to remain is color with rubber cement. Let dry and cover entire surface with rkest color. Let dry; then rub off the cement with an eraser for an teresting, three-color design.

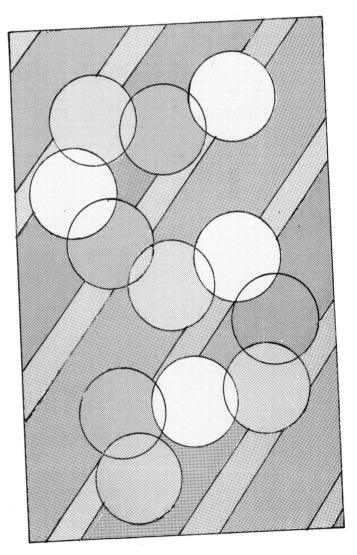

©1990 The Education Center, Inc.

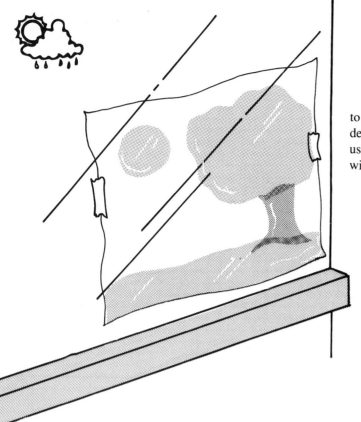

Plastic Wrap Pictures

Instead of another crayon and paper activity, treat your students to something different. Tape a piece of plastic wrap to each child's desk. Have the students draw their pictures on the plastic wrap using permanent markers. Tape the finished pictures on your windows for a stained-glass effect.

Pinecone Pictures

All you need to create unusual, three-dimensional pictures are pinecones, clear-drying glue, poster board, paint or crayons, and a pair of pliers. Draw a simple picture on the poster board. Remove the scales from the pinecones by hand or with the pliers. Glue the scales to the poster board to make interesting creatures and designs. Add additional details with paint or crayons.

Watercolor Surprise

No two paintings will look alike when you use this inventive technique. On a large sheet of art paper, have each student drizzle white glue randomly. (Or have students use glue which has been tinted black with tempera paint.) A day or two later, have each student prepare his paper for painting by spraying it with water or dipping it in water. Using watercolor paints, have students paint their papers. Encourage students to let the colors mingle to create unique effects.

©1990 The Education Center, Inc.

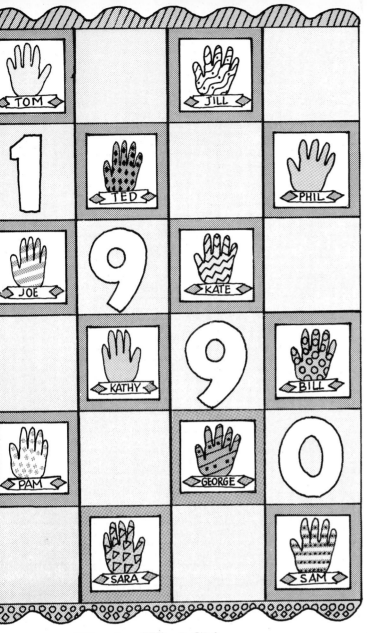

Class Quilt

Create a warm, classroom atmosphere with a colorful paper quilt representing each of your students. Give each child a 9" x 9" piece of construction paper. The student glues this piece of paper onto an 11" x 11" piece of black construction paper. He then traces his hand on "country print" wallpaper, cuts it out, and glues it in the center of his square. The student writes his name on a narrow strip of paper and glues it beneath his hand. Add small, black diamond shapes cut from construction paper as shown.

Design your quilt's pattern depending on the number of students. For example, you may wish to alternate solid black squares with the students' squares. Glue each square on butcher paper for backing, and add a scalloped wallpaper border and the year.

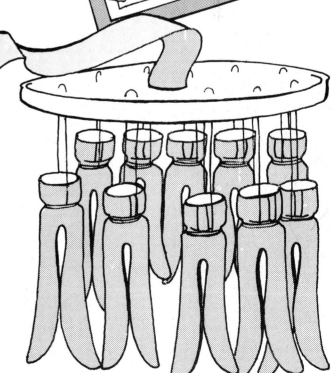

Wooden Wind Chimes

Enjoy gentle breezes with wind chimes made from wooden clothespins.

Materials for each student:
- ten round-head clothespins
- bright enamel paint
- large, plastic margarine tub lid
- 14" piece of ribbon
- ten 10" strands of fishing line
- small nail

Directions:
1. Paint the clothespins and let dry.
2. Use a nail to make ten pairs of holes 3/4" to 1" from the lid's edge.
3. For each pair of holes, insert fishing line up through the bottom of the lid, over the top, then down through the second hole. Tie a knot.
4. Tie each strand tightly around a clothespin head. Clothespins should hang at about the same height.
5. Poke a hole in the center of the lid and attach a ribbon for hanging.

©1990 The Education Center, Inc.

Colorful Impact

Color is the key to the visual appeal of this art activity, but you'll appreciate the eye-hand coordination practice your students will get, too. To begin, color a sheet of paper in stripes of alternating colors. Press down with the crayons a little more than usual to coat the paper heavily with color. From a coloring book, tear a design and place it faceup atop a white sheet of paper. Place these sheets atop the colored page. Tape the pages together before tracing the coloring book design with a pencil. Remind students to press down firmly as they're tracing. Carefully remove the tape and display the colorful design.

Sand Painting

Entice your students to create exotic sand paintings with this simple method. You will need glue, pencils, toothpicks, paintbrushes, heavy cardboard sheets (such as panels cut from shipping boxes), sand, and several colors of powdered tempera paint. To create a sand-painting medium, mix each color of tempera with sand. Sketch a design onto a sheet of cardboard before using toothpicks (for fine lines) and paintbrushes (for larger spaces) to apply glue to each section to bear a particular color. Pour sand of that color atop the glue, allow to dry, and shake off the excess sand. Continue gluing and adding sand for each color in the painting. An aluminum pop top ring may be glued to the back of the painting for hanging. The unusual texture created by the sand makes this project an excellent culminating activity for a unit on plants, flowers, the desert, Native Americans, or the Wild West.

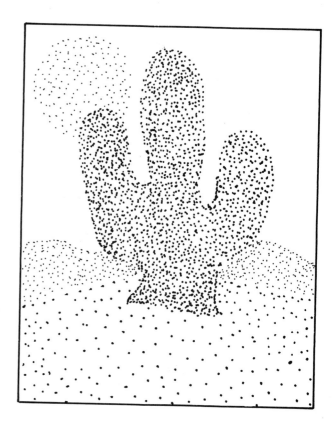

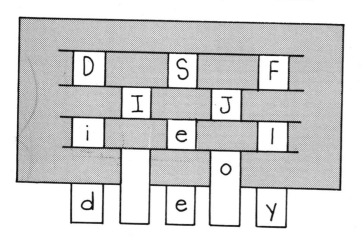

Secret Weaving

Take weaving a step further and turn it into a game of secret messages. Each child weaves a simple placemat from construction paper. When finished, the child pulls each strip down one block and writes a message as shown. When the weaving is back in place, the message is hidden. Pull the strips, and the secret upper-/lowercase message appears.

©1990 The Education Center, Inc.

Don't Worry, Be Happy

Since smiley faces are unmistakable symbols of happiness, your youngsters will pick up on the cheerful mood set by these bright grins. In preparation for the project, cut vegetables (such as potatoes, eggplants, cucumbers) in half, and fill each of several shallow pans with tempera paint. Dip each vegetable in paint before pressing it repeatedly onto art paper. Repeat with other vegetables. When dry, add facial features to each circle using markers. To use as a mobile, cut a 10" circle from the printed art paper, and back with another similarly prepared 10" circle. Using bright ribbon, suspend several of these two-sided circles at varying heights.

Circle Pictures

Don't toss those tubes! Use cardboard tubes from bathroom tissue, paper towels, or wrapping paper for this art project. Cut each tube into several sections. Provide art paper and several colors of tempera paint.

Students dunk cardboard tube pieces in paint and press them onto their papers to create unusual creatures. Features may be added with crayons or markers.

May I Have A Letter?

Need a quick and easy art project for a Friday afternoon? Then give new life to old bulletin board letters! Give one letter to each student. Challenge the student to glue the letter in any position on a piece of art paper. The student then uses crayons or markers to draw a picture incorporating the letter in a unique way. What a fun way to stretch your students' imaginations!

©1990 The Education Center, Inc.

141

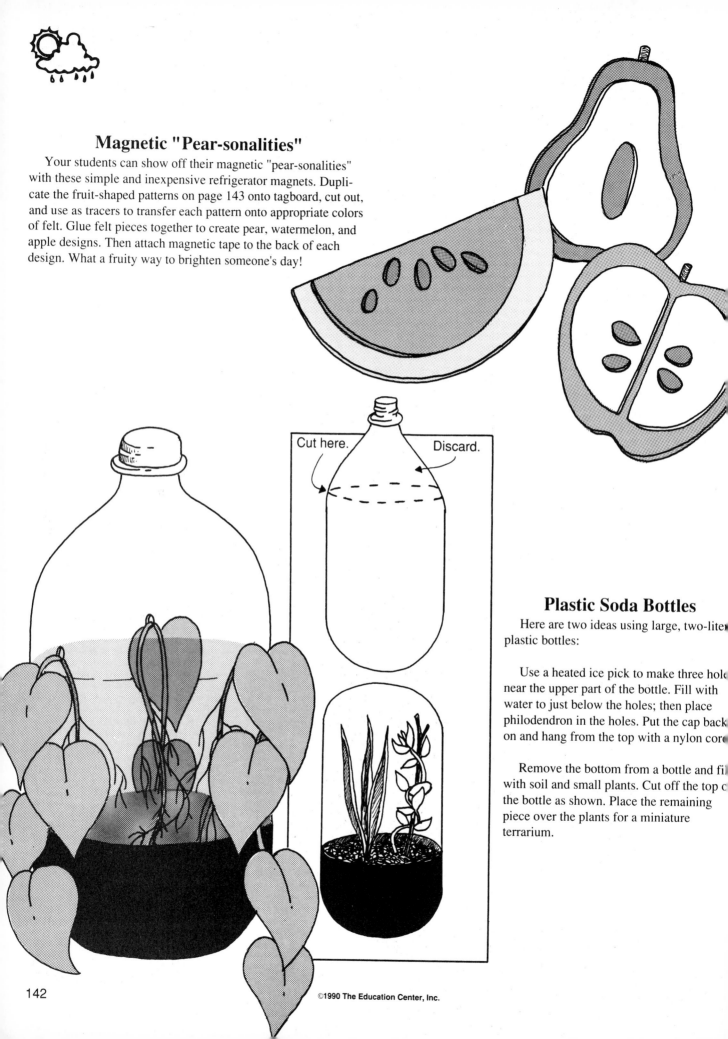

Magnetic "Pear-sonalities"

Your students can show off their magnetic "pear-sonalities" with these simple and inexpensive refrigerator magnets. Duplicate the fruit-shaped patterns on page 143 onto tagboard, cut out, and use as tracers to transfer each pattern onto appropriate colors of felt. Glue felt pieces together to create pear, watermelon, and apple designs. Then attach magnetic tape to the back of each design. What a fruity way to brighten someone's day!

Cut here.

Discard.

Plastic Soda Bottles

Here are two ideas using large, two-liter plastic bottles:

Use a heated ice pick to make three hole near the upper part of the bottle. Fill with water to just below the holes; then place philodendron in the holes. Put the cap back on and hang from the top with a nylon cor

Remove the bottom from a bottle and fil with soil and small plants. Cut off the top o the bottle as shown. Place the remaining piece over the plants for a miniature terrarium.

©1990 The Education Center, Inc.

atterns

e these patterns with "Magnetic 'Pear-sonalities' " on page 142.

Pear Patterns

Cut from green felt.

cut seed from brown felt

Cut from yellow felt.

Apple Patterns

Cut from
red felt.

Cut from white
felt.

Cut from white
felt.

Cut seeds from brown felt.

Watermelon Patterns

Cut from green felt.

Cut from pink felt.

Cut seeds from
brown felt.

©1990 The Education Center, Inc.

143

Alphabet Art

Cut block letters from large pieces of oaktag or poster board. Give one letter to each student. Children decorate their letters with markers or crayons, adding dots, shapes, flowers, or other designs. Mount the finished letters on assorted colors of construction paper.

Wild Weed Pocket

Tuck some dried weeds into paper pockets to emphasize nature's artistry. Begin by collecting dried weeds for the project. Then snip the sides of a U-shaped construction paper pocket as shown. Decorate the pocket using markers or crayons. Glue it to a contrasting sheet of construction paper, being certain to leave the pocket open at the top. Tape a bouquet of weeds at the stems and tuck them inside the pocket. Display these wild weed pockets side by side on a bulletin board or in a hallway for maximum impact.

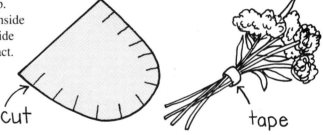

cut   tape

Plastic Wrap Sun Catchers

Brighten up your classroom with student-made sun catchers.

Materials: assorted colors of tissue paper, plastic wrap, white glue, yarn, scissors, tape, small pieces of cardboard, paintbrushes

Procedure:
1. Tear or cut tissue paper into small pieces.
2. Tape a piece of plastic wrap to a piece of cardboard.
3. Paint an area of the plastic wrap with white glue.
4. Lay pieces of tissue on the glue, overlapping the pieces. Carefully paint over the tissue with white glue. Allow to dry overnight.
5. Peel tissue paper away from the plastic wrap. Cut out a design such as a circle or star. Glue yarn around the edge.
6. Add a yarn loop at the top and hang in a window. Let the sun shine through.

©1990 The Education Center, Inc.

Mirror Images

Hang these shiny pictures for an eye-catching display. Glue a 9" x 12" piece of aluminum foil to a piece of lightweight cardboard. Cut a 9" x 12" sheet of colorful construction paper in half on the diagonal. Cut designs along the center edge of one half of the construction paper, flipping the cut-out pieces over. Glue the pieces to the foil as shown to create a mirror image.

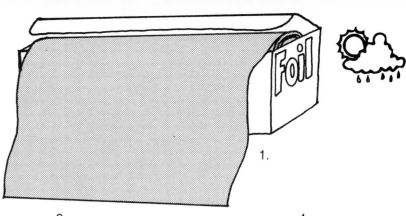

1.

2.

construction paper

12"

9"

3.

4.

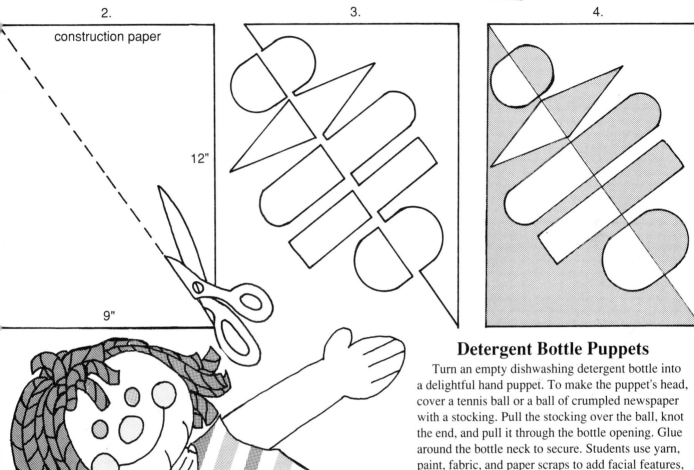

Detergent Bottle Puppets

Turn an empty dishwashing detergent bottle into a delightful hand puppet. To make the puppet's head, cover a tennis ball or a ball of crumpled newspaper with a stocking. Pull the stocking over the ball, knot the end, and pull it through the bottle opening. Glue around the bottle neck to secure. Students use yarn, paint, fabric, and paper scraps to add facial features, clothes, and arms. Cut off the base of the bottle so a hand can fit inside.

©1990 The Education Center, Inc.

Colorful Creations

Your students can experience color mixing firsthand while they create these colorful art projects. Drop primary colors of thinned tempera paint onto a flattened-out coffee filter. Observe as the colors blend to create secondary colors. Suspend each student's filter from the ceiling for a splash of color. Or staple filters to a bulletin board and add construction paper stems to create the illusion of a gigantic flower garden.

Bright Birds

Welcome a flock of bright birds into your classroom. Duplicate the parrot on page 147 on white paper for each child in your class. Soak the paper in water before having the student paint the parrot with bright watercolors. The children will enjoy watching the colors blend and bleed together in interesting patterns. After drying, have students use glue to outline their pictures in black yarn. Cut out the parrots. Hang from a clothesline or post on a bulletin board.

Marble Art

Save this fun project for a wet-weather day. Place gift box (without the lid), paint, a spoon, and several marbles at an art center. A student places a piece of art paper (cut to size) in the box. After dropping the marbles in paint, the student spoons them on the pape and tilts the box. The rolling marbles will make a unique and colorful design on the paper. Be sure to provide a bowl of water in which to clean the marble after each picture. To vary, use golf balls, spools, or acorns.

146

©1990 The Education Center, Inc.

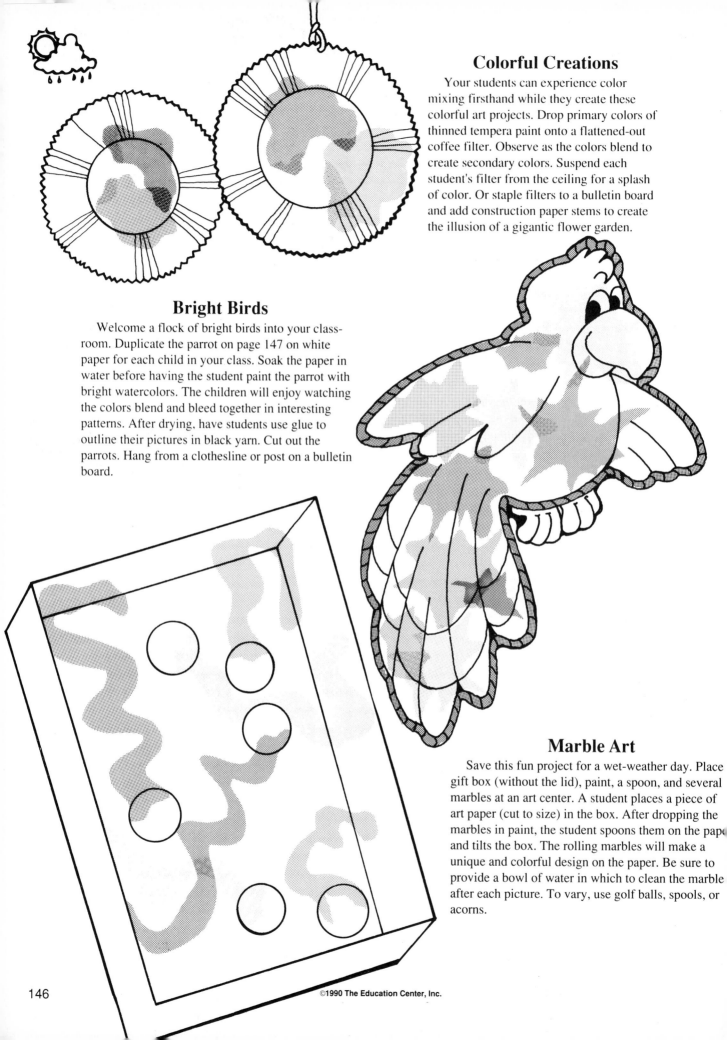

©1990 The Education Center, Inc.

Funny Face

Everyone loves clowns, so why not fill your classroom with their funny faces? Cut a large oval from a light-colored piece of construction paper. Glue it to a larger piece of construction paper to make the clown's face. Dampen the face with a sponge; then add features with colored chalk. When dry, complete your happy clown face using glue, buttons, felt, fabric scraps, and yarn.

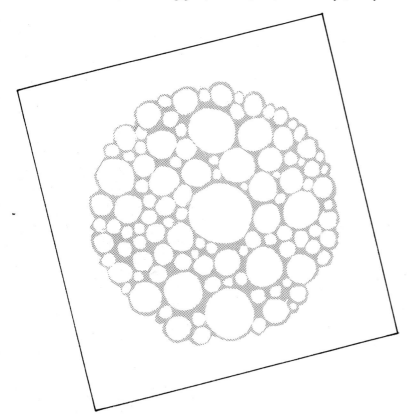

Bubble Prints

Prints from bubbles make an unusual art activity—and lots of warm-weather fun if done outside! Combine tempera paint with a small amount of liquid detergent in a bowl. Using a straw, blow bubbles into the mixture until they reach over the rim. Place a sheet of paper over the top of the bowl. Remove the paper to see a colorful bubble print!

Crayon Batik

Batik is a textile craft that lends itself to interesting effects with crayons. To experiment with this art method in your classroom, use bright crayons to draw and color a design on a piece of white art paper. Place the drawing in a pan of water. Remove after a couple of minutes. Gently ball up the picture to crinkle the paper. Flatten out the drawing on dry newspaper. Paint one shade of watercolor over the entire drawing. Quickly dip it back into the water. Remove and allow to dry flattened out on newspaper.

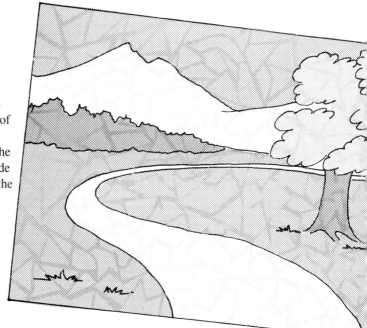

©1990 The Education Center, Inc.

Country Bookmarks

Here's a touch of country to add to your reading program! Provide each child with a black, construction paper strip and three construction paper quilt squares. (Small-print gift wrap works great here, too!) Students add "stitching," as shown, to the squares and glue in place. Laminate. To complete, students punch holes in the tops and add colorful tassels made from yarn.

Warm Fuzzy Pencils

A fuzzy friend resting on your pencil will brighten any school day. Wrap a bright orange or green pipe cleaner around the eraser end of a pencil as shown. Glue wiggly eyes to the end of the pipe cleaner. Turn your warm fuzzy pencil into a beetle by adding paper antennae.

Custom Coloring

Do your children enjoy coloring as a free-time activity? Then make your own coloring books! Have students use black crayons to draw simple pictures on white or manila paper. Place these outline drawings in a folder. During free time, students can choose pictures from the folder to color. Children will have great fun seeing their friends coloring the pictures they drew.

©1990 The Education Center, Inc.

Wall Plaques

Students will be pleased to take home these easy-to-make wall plaques. For each wall plaque you will need:

tile	Diamond Dust
picture from a greeting card	12" of ribbon, two inches wide
Mod Podge	1 1/4" metal ring
scissors	glue
	paintbrush

Have each student cut out his greeting card picture. Next the student paints Mod Podge onto his tile and lays the cutout on top, pressing down on the picture to assure that it is firmly attached. Let dry for 15 to 20 minutes. Repeat this step, letting each layer of Mod Podge dry, until desired finish is achieved. Before the final coat is dry, sprinkle with Diamond Dust and shake off the excess. Slide the metal ring onto the ribbon and fold ribbon in half. Glue the ribbon ends together and let dry. When dry, glue the ribbon to the plaque to create a hanger.

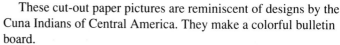

Step 1	Step 2	Step 3

Cuna Indian Pictures

These cut-out paper pictures are reminiscent of designs by the Cuna Indians of Central America. They make a colorful bulletin board.

Materials: 9" x 12" construction paper, paper clips, X-acto knife, glue, felt-tipped pens or crayons.

Procedure:

1. Draw a basic design on construction paper, making sure to leave a one-inch border all around and allowing your design to touch the border. See illustration #1. Cut out the inside shapes with an X-acto knife.
2. Place this pattern over the next color of construction paper. Use paper clips to keep papers from shifting. Trace and cut out the inner design 1/4" from the inside edges. Place this cutout on top of the next color of paper.
3. Continue this subtractive process with three or more colors of paper. Layer each piece of paper behind the others to show depth and pattern structure.
4. Use small amounts of glue to anchor layers together.

©1990 The Education Center, Inc.

Paper Clip Jewelry

Make simple jewelry out of common school supplies. Provide each student with approximately 30 paper clips. Use colored tape that is one inch wide. Link paper clips together to make necklaces, bracelets, headbands, pins, and belts. Wrap pieces of colored tape around the clips to create different designs and patterns.

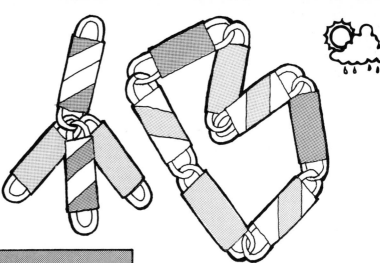

Larger-than-Life Cartooning

Convert your classroom into Cartoon Town for an art class with surprising results. Enlarge or reduce a colorful cartoon or coloring-book scene to three inches square. (You will need one scene for every nine children in your class.) Draw a one-inch grid over the scene, and cut on the lines. Distribute these pieces at random to students. On a six-inch paper square, instruct each student to precisely enlarge his design to match and color. Youngsters will be fascinated with the results when the completed squares are positioned to reveal the picture.

Pasta Hot Rods

Your students will zoom to the art center to construct these creative cars. Provide glue and a supply of different shapes of pasta (wheels, spaghetti, corkscrews, fettucine, etc.). Each child glues the pasta together to make his own custom car. Let the cars dry overnight. The next day place the cars on newspaper and spray with paint. Have each child write a story about his hot rod to display with his creative vehicle.

©1990 The Education Center, Inc.

Don't Toss Those Tubes!

Your youngsters can design an entire parade of animal puppets using empty paper towel tubes.

Materials Needed:
1 lid from a 13-oz. coffee can
construction paper
glue
scissors
a paper towel tube for each student
stapler
two 2" x 9" construction paper strips for each child

Procedure:
1. Staple closed one end of each tube.
2. Trace the coffee can lid on construction paper. Cut out this circle for the puppet face.
3. Glue on construction paper pieces for facial features.
4. Glue back of each puppet face to the closed end of the tube.
5. Glue two 2" x 9" construction paper strips together around each tube for arms. When the glue is dry, trim ends to represent paws or fingers.

Paper Plate Personalities

Here's a puppet design that is perfect for creating monsters, space creatures, or goofy characters. The secret to success with these puppets is to provide a multitude of construction materials—the more bizarre and colorful, the better.

Materials Needed:
1 1/2 paper plates per child
stapler
craft glue
scissors
construction paper
any assortment of the following materials:

tissue paper	crepe paper
giftwrapping paper	foil
egg carton sections	cellophane
yarn	pipe cleaners
buttons	fabric scraps
sewing notions	

Procedure:
1. Select and prepare material for your puppet's hair.
2. Staple and/or glue a paper plate to a half plate, fastening in your choice of "hair." Allow for drying time if glue is used.
3. Select materials for facial features and accessories and glue these onto the puppet.

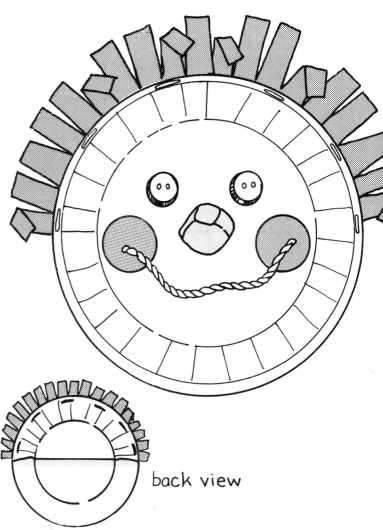

back view

152

©1990 The Education Center, Inc.

Fishbowl Fun

Trace a fishbowl pattern (see below) on a folded piece of waxed paper; then cut out the two bowls. Cut fish (see patterns below) and plants from construction paper, adding details with crayons or markers. Arrange the fish and plants on one of the bowls. Add crayon chips to the bottom of the bowl. Place the other bowl on top and press with a warm, protected iron until sealed. Display the bowls in the windows or hang them from the ceiling.

Use the fish for "Goldfish Bowls" on page 156 also.

Patterns

©1990 The Education Center, Inc.

Paper Plate Samplers

Cross-stitched, paper plate samplers make a super display. Have each student design a cross-stitch picture on graph paper, then transfer the X marks to a paper plate using a pencil. The child then makes the actual stitches in the plate with a needle and yarn or thread. Have students add yarn borders and hangers to their samplers before displaying the projects in a class gallery.

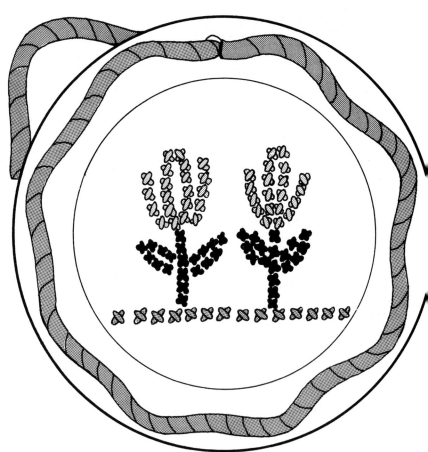

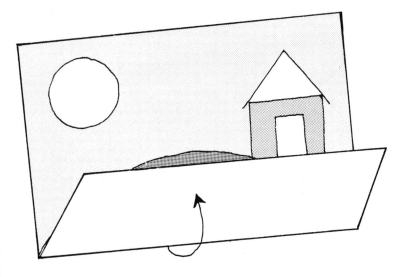

Landscape Reflections

After folding back the bottom third of a piece of paper, paint a landscape picture on the remaining paper with thick tempera. Unfold the bottom and press against the painting while the paint is still wet. Pull down the flap to reveal a reflection of the landscape as it would be seen in a lake or pond.

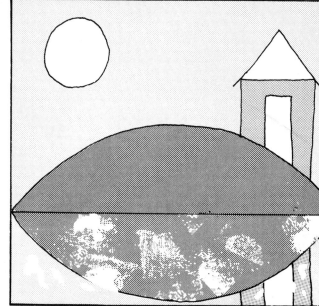

154 ©1990 The Education Center, Inc.

Clay Another Way

Clay is available in a marvelous variety of colors, and there's more than one way to turn students' imaginations loose with it. One way for students to use clay is to draw with it. The residue left on the paper has a pleasant effect, and using several colors on a project yields appealing results. Another method is to have students put small dabs of clay on art paper, and then press and rub them out in several directions. Now that's creative artwork!

Towel Art

For beautiful, three-dimensional pictures, tear off a paper towel! Draw a picture on a piece of art paper. Fill in the picture with pieces of paper towels that have been torn, cut, twisted, or braided. After gluing the paper towel pieces to the picture, color them with paint, markers, or dyes. Since the toweling is very absorbent, your picture will be colorful in no time!

Tissue Paper Art

Brighten up your winter classroom with this colorful art project. Small pieces of brightly colored tissue paper and thinned, white glue create an interesting effect. Have students tear tissue paper apart. Lightly coat a sheet of white drawing paper with thinned glue. Have students arrange the pieces of tissue paper on the glue-covered sheet. Encourage students to overlap the pieces to achieve a mixture of colors. Pieces of shredded yarn placed under the tissue paper help create a different look. Have each student brush a coating of thinned glue over the tissue paper and let it dry. For a nice finish, coat the picture with glossy acrylic spray.

©1990 The Education Center, Inc.

Goldfish Bowls

Turn two paper plates into a colorful fishbowl! Cut out the center of one paper plate. Paint the back of the resulting "frame"; then glue clear plastic wrap over the hole on the other side. Paint the inside of the second plate blue. After drying, glue colored sand on one-third of the blue side and shake off the excess. Use the patterns on page 153 to make goldfish from orange construction paper. For a 3-D effect, fringe the tails and bend the heads and tails forward before gluing. Add green paper seaweed, red coral, yellow starfish, etc. To finish the fishbowl, place the inside edges of the two plates together and glue.

Tissue Paper Pictures

Add color to your windows with these works of art. Fold a sheet of black construction paper in half and cut out the center to make a frame. Cut various colors of tissue paper in different shapes and sizes. Apply glue to the edges of each piece of tissue paper and, one by one, glue them to each other, beginning in a corner on the back of the frame. You may wish to overlap some pieces more than others. Turn the picture over when the frame is completely filled in with tissue and the glue has dried. Use black construction paper scraps to make cutouts to paste over the tissue to create a silhouette effect. Tape finished projects on a window.

156

©1990 The Education Center, Inc.

Paper Plate Art

These art projects are a feast for the eyes when displayed together, and they are a great introduction to the concepts of positive and negative space. Have each student sketch a scene in the middle of a lightweight paper plate. Using an X-acto knife, have him cut away portions of the drawing which will define the positive and negative space. Have students erase any remaining pencil marks. Mount the finished projects on a bulletin board covered with black paper to create an eye-catching exhibit.

Milk Carton Computers

Children will enjoy making these "computers" and programming them with ~~ning games. Students prepare cards with questions on one side and answers on ~~other. When they insert a "floppy disk" (question-side-up) in the top slot, it ~~es out the bottom slot with the answer showing!

~~erials: one half-gallon milk carton, scissors, 9" x 3" poster board strip, tape, ~~truction paper, Con-tact paper (optional), cards

~~ctions:

Open the folded top of the milk carton. Cut down one side and across the bottom to form a door.

Cut two 1/2-inch-wide slots on the door as shown. (One slot should be at the top of the carton right below the fold. The other slot should be at the bottom.)

Position the poster board strip between the slots as shown. Tape the strip to the top of the upper slot and the bottom of the lower slot.

Close the door and tape the cut edges.

Refold the top of the carton and tape. Cover the carton with Con-tact paper or construction paper. Decorate your computer, and program a set of cards with review questions on one side and answers on the other.

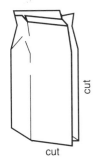

cut

cut

2.

two slots

3.

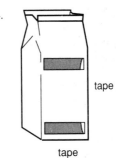

poster board

4.

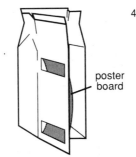

tape

tape

5.

©1990 The Education Center, Inc.

Anytime Art Recipes

Expand your classroom palette with these recipes. Create experimental batches of paint, putty, papier-mâché, or dough, and let students discover new ways to use them.

Homemade Play Dough

Homemade play dough works as well as the expensive brand from toy stores.

1 cup flour	1 cup water
1/2 cup salt	1 teaspoon vegetable oil
2 teaspoons cream of tartar	food coloring

Mix the dry ingredients. Then add the remaining ingredients and stir. In a heavy skillet, cook the mixture for two to three minutes, stirring frequently. Knead the dough until it becomes soft and smooth. Stir up several colors and store them in icing tubs.

No-cook Modeling Dough

No pots and pans are required for this concoction.

2 cups flour	food coloring or tempera paint
1 cup salt	2 tablespoons vegetable oil
water	(optional)

Mix the ingredients. Add oil unless you want the dough artwork to harden.

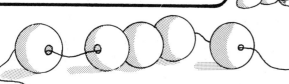

Baking Dough By The Batch

Make a batch of baking dough with this recipe.

2 cups flour
1 cup salt
water

Mix enough water with the dry ingredients to make a dough. After students create their masterpieces, bake the dough at 300° for about an hour—longer if the object is thick.

Baking Dough

Your students will enjoy creating dough designs for jewelry, refrigerator magnets, or other decorations. They'll also love the fact that they can measure and mix the dough recipe on their own.

4 tablespoons flour
1 tablespoon salt
2 tablespoons water

Have each student mix and knead the ingredients. Students may create their dough designs by rolling the dough flat with a rolling pin and using cookie cutters. Bake the dough at 350° for 1 to 1 1/2 hours. Students may then paint and shellac the designs.

©1990 The Education Center, Inc.

Dazzling Tempera Paints

If you want brighter colors, paint that doesn't run when used at the easel, and easy cleanup, use the following recipe:

    2 cups dry tempera paint
    1 cup liquid starch
    1 cup liquid soap (Clear or white works
      best.)

Mix the paint and soap; then add starch and stir. If the mixture becomes too thick, add more liquid soap. Don't add water. Store the paint mixture in one-pound coffee cans with plastic lids.

Corn Syrup Paint

Add food coloring to light corn syrup for a beautiful paint with an interesting texture. Mix up a cup of blue, yellow, and red, and put a spoonful of each on a paper plate for each student. Students paint their plates with the colors. Allow five days for drying time. Have each student trace a design onto the bottom of his plate and cut out the design.

Easy Dye

Here's a quick and easy way to dye macaroni, rice, beans, and seeds for art projects. In individual containers, pour a small amount of rubbing alcohol and tint to desired shades with food coloring. Drop the objects to be dyed into the liquid, let sit a minute, and then spoon out onto waxed paper. The alcohol evaporates quickly, leaving dyed objects ready for art.

Soap Flakes Finger Paint

Out of finger paint? Try this recipe for a homemade variety.

    1 1/2 cups dry laundry starch
    water
    1 1/2 cups soap flakes
    1 quart boiling water
    food coloring or tempera paint

Mix starch with enough cold water to make a paste. Add boiling water and stir until clear. Cool and add soap flakes and coloring. Store in a tightly sealed container.

©1990 The Education Center, Inc.

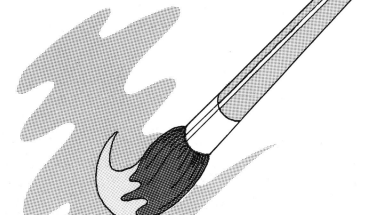

Papier-Mâché

For an easy papier-mâché glue, mix equal parts of liquid starch and cold water. Tear strips of newspaper, and dip these in the mixture before applying to a form of chicken wire or rolled newspaper.

Shiny Paint

1 part white liquid glue
1 part tempera paint
Mix ingredients. Apply with a brush or experiment with other methods. Shiny paint gives a wet look.

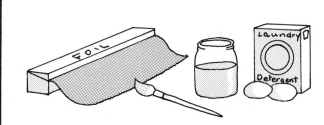

Egg Finger Paint

Mix a little egg yolk, dry detergent, and food coloring to make a paint that sticks to surfaces such as glass, aluminum foil, or freezer paper.

Magic Putty

2 parts regular white Elmer's Glue
(not Elmer's School Glue)
1 part liquid starch
Mix ingredients. Let dry in air. Have students experiment with it and write down their observations: it bounces, it stretches, it lifts pictures from newspapers and magazines! Store in an airtight container.

Salt Paint

2 teaspoons salt
1 teaspoon liquid starch
a few drops of tempera paint
Mix the ingredients together. Apply with a brush. Salt paint adds an "icy" touch to winter pictures.

160

©1990 The Education Center, Inc.